"The discipline of Enterprise Architecture is comprised of synthesis, analysis, and strategy. It involves taking the best thinking that the industry has, marrying it with a mercurial technology landscape, and overlaying an ephemeral business strategy in order to generate clarity of direction that paves the way to execution. Suresh is able to take the reader on the journey from EA framework selection through strategic planning by integrating current EA thinking with years of practical experience. This book is a great reference for executives trying to quantify the value of EA, new EA practitioners seeking to understand the history of the field, or seasoned EA veterans seeking a new perspective."

—Joseph Blaszczak, Senior MTS, Director Enterprise Architecture, T-Mobile, USA

"This is a very valuable book that I wish I had in my hands years ago when I was an aspiring young architect, trying to find my place in the enterprise and do my job the best way possible. It would have saved me lots of headaches, confusion, and futile fights in my career. This book raises awareness of Enterprise Architecture among professionals in the industry, aligns their expectations, and puts it in a proper perspective. Just like a linguist, the author has found the most versatile language to build a common ground for that understanding and convey the principles and basics of Enterprise Architecture in a way fathomable by every actor in the enterprise. Through a series of real-life examples and approaches to structuring and presenting complex information in a concise manner, the author proves Enterprise Architecture is vital to achieving enterprise flexibility, sustainability, and in many cases survival. I recommend this book to all C-level professionals who need to know what a powerful tool Enterprise Architecture is, to all middle managers who wish to achieve better enterprise efficiency, and, of course, to all aspiring young architects trying to find their place in the enterprise and do their job the best way possible."

— Emanuil Donchev, CTO, Effortel Technologies SA

ARCHITECTING
ENTERPRISE
TRANSFORMATIONS

ARCHITECTING
ENTERPRISE
TRANSFORMATIONS

A HOLISTIC APPROACH
TO BUSINESS
OPTIMIZATION,
INNOVATION,
AND AGILITY

SURESH DONE

Advantage | Books

Published by Advantage, Charleston, South Carolina.
Member of Advantage Media.

ADVANTAGE is a registered trademark, and the Advantage colophon is a trademark of Advantage Media Group, Inc.

Printed in the United States of America.

10 9 8 7 6 5 4 3 2 1

ISBN: 978-1-64225-260-6 (Hardcover)
ISBN: 978-1-64225-454-9 (eBook)

LCCN: 2023903373

Cover design by Josh Frederick.
Interior design by Megan Elger.

This publication is designed to provide accurate and authoritative information in regard to the subject matter covered. It is sold with the understanding that the publisher is not engaged in rendering legal, accounting, or other professional services. If legal advice or other expert assistance is required, the services of a competent professional person should be sought.

Advantage Media helps busy entrepreneurs, CEOs, and leaders write and publish a book to grow their business and become the authority in their field. Advantage authors comprise an exclusive community of industry professionals, idea-makers, and thought leaders. Do you have a book idea or manuscript for consideration? We would love to hear from you at **AdvantageMedia.com**.

I would like to thank God the Almighty for giving me everything that I have right now, protecting me from evil, removing the obstacles that I encountered in my life, and paving the path for my success.

I want to thank my late parents for providing me good education, imbuing values and ethics in me, and making the person who I am right now.

I want to thank my family, my wife, Ananda, and my son, Nathan, for bearing and supporting my extreme hours of work and travel. Without them I would have not achieved what I did so far in my career.

I want to thank my friends, colleagues, relatives, and siblings for their support in my life. Everyone played a part in my achievements and sustainability.

Last but not the least, I would like to thank everyone who are associated with SNA Technologies, in one way or another, for your support and encouragement for the past seventeen years.

CONTENTS

A NEW BLUEPRINT

At some point, most of us have stood at the base of a skyscraper and stared up in awe at its towering form. There is a sense of wonder that not only was this building constructed but also that it started out as an idea, a few lines drawn on a blueprint. And then this blueprint was transformed through hundreds of hands and thousands of materials into reality.

Most business leaders I meet understand the premise and importance of architecture. They realize that before they can build, they need a design. They spend hours thinking about the purpose of the building, the exterior design, the layout of the interior, and how the building will benefit the business and enable them to fulfill their mission in a practical sense. The blueprint set in front of them by the architect makes the building feel real before even an ounce of concrete is poured for the foundation.

No doubt there is a very clear and tangible connection for leaders when they align the structural architecture with their business needs. They have to think about the square footage needed for staff, how many offices or cubicles are required, how much storage space is needed, where conference rooms and corner offices will be assigned. Therefore, it is not too challenging for leaders to think of the blueprint and not only imagine what will be built but also identify the best design for the enterprise's needs.

However, the problem I see most often among leaders is not one that concerns any physical building. Instead it boils down to a disconnect between how they design, plan, and implement *Enterprise* Architecture—that is, a thoughtfully considered framework of how the enterprise can not only carry out its best work but also enable transformation.

In short, companies need a new blueprint—one that will lay out all of the business needs, goals, and resources and align those to the long-term goals of the business. In other words, regardless of what kind of physical architecture the business inhabits, a more important question is what the Enterprise Architecture looks like. This encompasses everything from the desired state of the business to meet changes to what technology is needed to carry out business. After all, technology can help a business face many types of changes, whether they involve digital transformation, changes in the market, or even changes in customer expectations. This alignment of business and technology to transform the enterprise from its current state to a more optimal state is the primary purpose of Enterprise Architecture, or EA, as I will routinely refer to it throughout this book.

Since Enterprise Architecture is still a relatively new field, it deserves some explanation. My own journey with EA began over thirty years ago, when I was a postgraduate student in India working in civil engineering and architecture. In that job, I was applying artificial intelligence concepts to optimize the design of steel structures, long before AI was widely known as it is today.

While this preceded me becoming an Enterprise Architect myself, it is this central idea of optimization—finding the *best* way to accomplish a goal—that is at the heart of Enterprise Architecture. In that role, I was helping carry out the vision of a physical architect in constructing their design while using technology as a means to a better way of fulfilling the design. Looking back, I can see how this was laying the foundation for what I help businesses do every day.

After moving to the United States, I became a consultant and IT architect for Compuware, helping other major companies like General Motors optimize their tech solutions as IT became more essential to the efficiency and profitability of the company. One of the great advantages I received from my time at Compuware was gaining experience in helping diverse companies across many industries develop individualized solutions. I learned that, like many things in life, there is no such thing as a one-size-fits-all approach. Rather, the best solutions are tailor made to the organization. This requires more time and effort and certainly a more intimate understanding of the organization but proves to yield the greatest results and rewards. It was this realization coupled with my experience that led me to becoming a pioneer in the world of EA.

During my time at Compuware, I was part of a team hired by GM as Enterprise Architects to establish an EA practice there. Very few organizations were doing this at the time, so we were one of the first to perform this service on such a large scale. Up until that point, my work had always been focused on the IT components of a business, but I had seen how IT cannot be optimized on its own separate from other business structures—rather, it must be driven by the needs and goals of the business itself.

This made me realize that what we were doing was not enough moving forward. We needed a full-fledged, holistic approach to the emerging field of Enterprise Architecture. In 2006, after the GM project had concluded, I was subcontracted by DaimlerChrysler as an

Enterprise Architect, and it was then that I founded SNA Technologies, which would practice EA solutions in a holistic manner. Since then, we have been on the front lines of helping businesses of all sizes establish a framework of solutions to help them carry out their mission on a long-term basis and, ideally, to be prepared for the unexpected.

So as Enterprise Architects, our job is to help enterprises architect the best version of their business—and then guide its transformation into the new version of the business to better accomplish their long-term goals. This goes far beyond traditional architecture, which only looks at the building because a building is only one part of a business, and more and more, we see entrepreneurs launching businesses *without* a physical brick-and-mortar building per se. In our increasingly remote work world existing within a globalized economy, enterprises have to find new ways to adapt to business transformations to position themselves for success. Simply put, the goal of Enterprise Architecture is to help an enterprise find the right direction to that success—and inevitably, technology plays a huge role in that process.

It is one thing to know and implement IT solutions for an enterprise. It is a whole other matter to align those solutions in the most optimal way, to process through what tools will amplify the productivity of the team over time and understand what operational standards must be met. I have seen firsthand that there are intelligent people who know the latest technology and how to use it, but the real matter is whether or not these professionals and their clients have answered these core questions:

- Did we look at all the options available to the enterprise?

- Which option is the best one to meet the enterprise's needs?

- Are there any standards that must be followed?

- What will help the enterprise best adapt for the future?

Now let us return to the image of that skyscraper towering above us. In a similar way that the structural architect must think of every aspect of how the building is designed, the Enterprise Architect bears the weight of knowing every aspect of the client's needs to help their enterprise succeed. The holistic view is one that does not concentrate only on the IT aspects of the business but also incorporates the client's business plan, their products, the practical needs of the enterprise's various components, the view of the customer and their long-term goals, and the path of transformation to meet those goals.

A successful Enterprise Architect creates a better business plan by looking at how and what needs to be done to help the organization accomplish its goals, creating a full-fledged plan, and then ensuring that the solutions are built in a systematic way that will be long-standing, not just a temporary bandage for today's problem—or only focus on today's "shiniest" new piece of technology. Ultimately, this full-scale and systematic approach will help the enterprise become more Agile in finding solutions and optimizing as new changes come their way.

> The Enterprise Architect bears the weight of knowing every aspect of the client's needs to help their enterprise succeed.

One problem I see nowadays is that the EA conversation rarely begins at the level of the C-Suite. Too often, it is someone in middle management who wants to bring an EA strategy into their organization, and they must then struggle and fight an uphill battle to convince the C-Suite that it should be prioritized and is in the enterprise's best interest. Because EA is still a new concept and has not been a regular part of the business development conversation, it can be a challenge for the C-Suite to prioritize it in the same way that they would prioritize a blueprint for a new headquarters.

They believe the myth that technology is only for the "tech-savvy" people to make decisions about and silo it off into its own corner rather than seeing how it needs to be integrated with strategy. But if the C-Suite can champion the importance of EA and how a new blueprint for optimal business functioning can make the organization more streamlined, more efficient, and more productive, then there is a higher chance of success for everyone involved.

Enterprise Architecture can feel overwhelming, especially for executives who do not consider themselves tech savvy. But the good news is that you don't have to have all the answers or know everything because the EA process is designed to help guide you to the best answers for *your* enterprise.

As a pioneer in the field of Enterprise Architecture, my goal with this book is not to overwhelm you but rather to give you a practical overview of EA so that you can evaluate how a thoughtful and comprehensive EA plan can benefit your enterprise, no matter what size it is or what industry. I hope to remove some of the mystery and confusion around EA so that you can better grasp how various EA frameworks can be customized to make your enterprise more efficient, productive, and Agile. In short, you do not need to be tech savvy or have mountains of IT experience to understand EA; you only need to have the interest in how it can improve your business.

In the chapters that follow, we'll look at how to bridge the gap between the various disciplines of EA while also providing some guidance on how all aspects—from strategic planning to operational needs to the implementation of new applications—can be accomplished in a more seamless manner. Not only should this remove some of the stress from the strategic planning process, but it also should create a roadmap you can follow for future innovation.

In the current global climate, organizations need an effective EA strategy more than ever before, not as a one-time project but as an ongoing process in business planning. In fact, the most recent COVID-19 crisis has made it incredibly clear how vital EA has become as organizations, including the highest levels of government, had to quickly adjust and create new technology solutions to carry out essential functions in the face of the unexpected.

While this new blueprint will not lead to a shiny skyscraper that crowds will stand in awe of, it can lead to a better business design that you as a leader can be proud of. But just as a structural blueprint is expected to be acted upon, so is an EA blueprint. When executed properly, EA has the potential to not only increase an enterprise's effectiveness but also a leader's confidence in the work that is being accomplished day in, day out. Unlike traditional blueprints, the EA blueprint is alive, adapting to changes along the way and growing with the enterprise. It is not a finite project like a skyscraper, but it outlines an infinite path to continuous improvement.

CHAPTER 1

THE STATE OF ENTERPRISE ARCHITECTURE

A few years ago, we were approached by a new client facing a rather unique problem—or rather, a set of problems. For the sake of anonymity, I'm going to refer to them as Southeast Regional Bank. They were a regional bank that was made up of several businesses: a retail bank, a corporate bank, a lending company, and an insurance investments group, which was subdivided into an insurance products company and an investments company. To complicate things further, they were partnering with two external organizations: one for issuing credit cards and another assisting with the investments unit.

Their greatest concern was the fact that each of these units of the enterprise operated independently as separate silos that did not communicate or cross over with one another. As such, each unit had its own separate customers, differing business processes, and different technology being utilized, from their customer databases to office applications. In other words, there were many moving parts and no clear cohesion to those parts.

This snowballed into a laundry list of concerns: they had no holistic strategy, their financial reports were six months out of date, they had no single view of their customers and no management control, they were lacking in enterprise-wide leverage, and they desperately needed a review and update of their business requirements through a single architectural approach.

Their long-term view was to consolidate all these siloed units so that the enterprise could become a one-stop banking shop for customers utilizing a federated business model, standardizing their processes, and streamlining their financial reporting. Not only would this allow them to become more efficient, but it would also allow them to grow their business through a common customer view and bundling of products and services.

Now if that gives you a headache, then perhaps it is best I don't get more detailed since this is a simplification of their problems. After all, where does one even begin to unravel all these moving parts? How would they continue to serve customers and maintain profitability when so much transformation was needed?

Yet that is exactly the aim of Enterprise Architecture (EA).

If it is still a new term or concept for you, then you are in good company. When I inform people that I am an Enterprise Architect, it usually requires some clarification. For one thing, EA is a business discipline critical for strategic planning in which we focus on solving business problems while also centering on organizational alignment. While this includes the consideration of IT solutions, it looks beyond the technology itself and examines every component of an enterprise to optimize the organization as a whole. In other words, it's not about reinventing the wheel per se but making the wheel roll better and in the right direction.

When I founded SNA Technologies in 2006, I wanted to ensure that we would help our clients by customizing EA concepts to their organizational dynamics, culture, and long-term goals. This means developing an intimate knowledge of the clients' needs to not only guide them in the process but also to adapt EA strategies through action-based steps that will solve whatever problems they may be facing.

It's not about reinventing the wheel per se but making the wheel roll better and in the right direction.

As I introduce you to the world of EA throughout this book, we will return often to the story of Southeast Regional Bank and show how they applied an Enterprise Architecture strategy to help them streamline their processes, grow in efficiency and communication, and ultimately help them become more Agile and innovative in serving their customers.

The Basic Elements of Enterprise Architecture

In taking a holistic view of an organization, one must first understand that Enterprise Architecture can be divided into four architecture domains as described in the following chart:

DOMAIN	DESCRIPTION	ASKS	EXAMPLES
BUSINESS ARCHITECTURE	Defines the overall business strategy, governance, organization and structure, and key business services.	What does the enterprise want to accomplish? What is the enterprise's mission and vision?	Bank providing banking services, logistics company transporting and delivering goods, software company developing softwa
DATA ARCHITECTURE	Describes the structure of an organization's logical and physical data assets and its data management resources.	What data entities are needed to run the business? What data is needed to help the business grow?	Customer data in a Customer Manage ment System (CMS employee data maintained by HR, product data.
APPLICATION ARCHITECTURE	Provides a blueprint for the individual applications to be deployed within the business, their interactions, and their relationships to the enterprise's core processes.	What systems does the organization need to support the business, including business functions, staff needs, and service needs?	Customer Relation ship Management (CRM) systems like Salesforce, accounting softwa like QuickBooks, messenger tools li Microsoft Teams.
TECHNOLOGY ARCHITECTURE	Describes the logical software and hardware capabilities that are required to support the deployment of the business, data, and application architecture domains.	What technology infrastructure does the enterprise need to support the three upper domains?	IT infrastructure, middleware, networks, commur cations, processing standards.

While every enterprise can be broken down and assessed through these four domains, not every EA initiative will impact all four domains. Therefore, if a specific aspect of the business does not have any IT applications involved, it can be optimized without having to touch on the technology domain. But as we go through the EA process, you will see how these domains are often linked—and *should* be linked—when optimizing the enterprise.

These domains are especially important to keep in mind as we look at various Enterprise Architectures and reference architecture frameworks in the following chapters, especially since not all EA systems consider each domain equally. A "mature" architecture framework is one that considers all of these domains, while a "less mature" architecture framework may not.

Now back to the case of Southeast Regional Bank for a moment. From a business perspective, they had both external and internal drivers for change. Internal drivers for them included a desire to achieve cost efficiency and also cross-selling and bundling products, while there were also external drivers like customer demands, competition, laws and regulations, and market conditions.

Each of these drivers links to an enabler—that is, a solution that will enable each of the drivers. For example, take the driver of "cost efficiency" mentioned above. To achieve this, they would need to restructure automation systems, making it the enabler. In the case of the driver of "cross-selling products," they needed to have a 360-degree view of their customers, so they needed a CMS that would *enable* a single view of the customer.

Once we understand an enterprise's drivers and enablers, optimization begins with identifying the specific needs across the four domains. For the sake of simplifying things, we will just focus for now on Southeast Regional Bank's goal of improving the timeliness of their financial reporting.

- **Business:** Improve timeliness of financial reports from business units to corporate.

- **Data**: Synchronize data reporting systems across business units.

- **Application**: Research the applications that could be used for synchronization.

- **Technology**: Identify the specific tech that will be deployed for report synchronization.

From there, three *levels* of architecture are identified:

- First Level: Strategy Architecture—Enterprise Level

- Second Level: Segment Architecture—Divisions of the Enterprise (e.g., Human Resources, Sales, Customer Service)

- Third Level: Capability Architecture—Project Level (e.g., reorganization of a division, creation of new reporting process, deployment of new technology solutions, etc.)

These levels will define the Strategy Architecture Roadmap developed to segment the initiatives and construct a timeline of capabilities and work packages to be performed. In the case of Southeast Regional Bank, their roadmap consisted of a three-year plan to accomplish all of the initiatives and enterprise optimization. I hope that this fact alone is proof of how detail oriented and specific the process of architecting an enterprise is. It's not an overnight quick-fix project but a thorough and thoughtful process that can revitalize and empower the enterprise for the long term.

It's not an overnight quick-fix project but a thorough and thoughtful process that can revitalize and empower the enterprise for the long term.

The Evolution of Enterprise Architecture

Before we can discuss these elements in more detail and how they can impact *your* organization, I believe it's important to first show you the evolution of EA since its inception in the '90s up to its current state today. As I see it, there have been three stages in the evolution of Enterprise Architecture, each one of them prompted by a financial crisis occurring in the modern tech era.

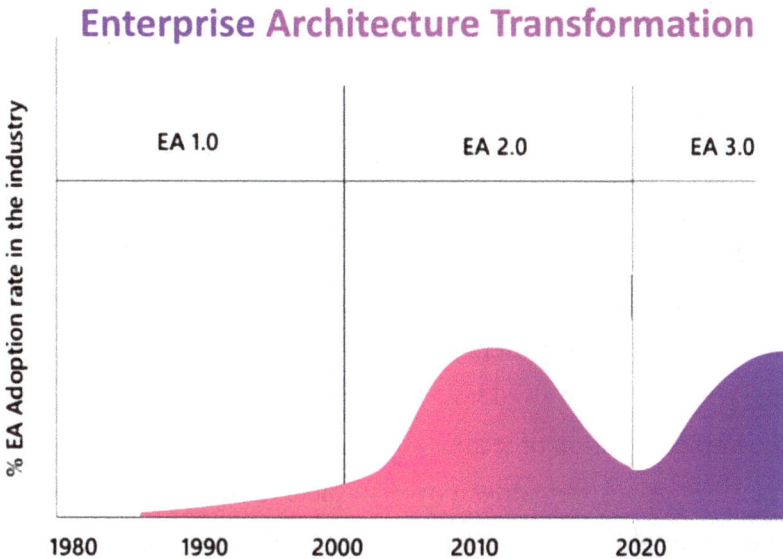

Enterprise Architecture Transformation

EA 1.0   EA 2.0   EA 3.0

% EA Adoption rate in the industry

1980   1990   2000   2010   2020

These stages are most easily marked by the "dot-com bubble burst" of the early 2000s and the Great Recession of 2008. Each of these crises, as difficult as they were, has served as proof that organizations with an established EA strategy are more adaptable and therefore more likely to survive that crisis.

ENTERPRISE ARCHITECTURE 1.0: LATE 1980s TO 2000

The '80s and '90s were a massive turning point for the intersection of technology in both personal and professional settings. This era saw advancements in telecommunication, the normalization of the PC in middle-class homes, the birth of the internet, and new software applications like Windows 95, which standardized workplace functions for greater efficiency. It is this collection of changes that gave birth to the concept of Enterprise Architecture.

More than anything else, this time period marked an overlapping of business and technology not dissimilar to the Industrial Revolution, when businesses willing to "upgrade" could move ahead and those failing to adapt fell behind or were replaced by more innovative enterprises. Ultimately, this era was one when IT had all the money and the power, as the business sector listened to IT rather than the other way around.

As such, this phase of EA was predominantly focused on the domain of technology architecture and how to integrate tech solutions into the business on an ad hoc basis. There was no planning involved in the implementation of technology, no strategic planning—enterprise transformations were driven by a simple eagerness to implement the latest technology available. As such, the predominant line of thinking was that if the business had the money to build or incorporate IT systems, then they did so.

Typically, this meant that the EA planning—if it was happening at all—was only occurring at the Business Level and would not necessarily "trickle down" to the implementation or Operational Level of the enterprise. This era was defined as a very siloed view of the enterprise, which was focused purely on optimizing the technology infrastructure in which the top-level execs may have had a plan, but it was not communicated well throughout the layers of the organization, nor was there always a clear purpose in the changes being made.

Therefore, the implementation of new technology didn't always work and could actually lead to inefficiencies since the strategies were ill conceived or forced upon workers without explanation on the "why" of the new technology. For example, the C-Suite may have been clear and unified among themselves about the advantages of the new technology, so they assumed that middle management and the lower levels of the business would automatically understand these advantages too. In that process, the strategies and purpose were lost in translation, and ultimately, the actual implementation of the technology ended up being different from what leadership originally had in mind.

For example, let's imagine for a moment that it's 1996, and a midsized manufacturer decides to implement and launch a company-wide email system because they have some surplus in the budget to try something new, and the COO has had some positive experience with personal email. For upper-level management, the advantages of this are obvious: communication between departments can be sped up, and they can document correspondence within the company with a higher level of efficiency and transparency. As such, they make assumptions that the rest of the company will understand this.

However, some members of middle management dislike the change, and they see nothing wrong with the old way of doing things. To them, it seems like not only an unnecessary expense but also a disruption to productivity, as they have to learn a new system in which they have to type in login credentials, type the message, and wait for the reply, instead of just picking up the phone to call someone's direct extension as they have always done. To them, it just feels like the executives are making it harder for them to get their job done.

Over time, upper management grows frustrated that lower levels won't use their email, and the lower levels complain to each other about "corporate interference," furthering the divide between management and staff, leading to loss of productivity and turnover issues.

Yes, in the end, email will win and be adopted by all members of the organization, but the implementation will be slower than intended by the C-Suite and with more bumps and conflict than if they only had spent the time to develop a strategy and invested more time in communicating that strategy. These are the types of "growing pains" that showed the necessity for a more fully realized Enterprise Architecture through developing a blueprint for implementation that could align new technology with business processes and procedures.

As you will see, this initial phase of EA was lacking in several key components that would come into later phases, including the following:

- Documentation to translate these strategies at all levels of the enterprise

- Identification of the building blocks needed to accomplish the strategies

- Methods to prove the assessment of those strategies to mitigate the potential risks before embarking on the implementation

ENTERPRISE ARCHITECTURE 2.0: 2000 TO 2020

As the new millennium arrived with its fears of Y2K, enterprises of all shapes and sizes were implementing technology into every aspect of their business. EA was still in its infancy, as organizations developed their own methods for incorporating technology—but with no holistic view for doing so.

Then came the infamous "dot-com burst," which led to a sudden hesitancy among leaders in how they would implement technology moving forward. People started to look into EA a little bit more seriously, as they wanted to make sure they optimized their IT options through more thoughtful processes and decision making. Business leaders realized their IT expenditures were humongous and that they were spending too much on IT.

With this realization came another: that there was no way to optimize IT without optimizing the business, since the purpose of IT was to enable the business. Rather than automatically taking their cues from the IT industry, as had occurred in the '90s, leaders started to consider what the business was trying to accomplish and then develop IT systems aligned to those business needs.

This helped lead to the rise of the modern IT professional, as it couldn't be expected for a C-level executive to make all tech decisions for a company and keep up to date with the rapid changes occurring in technology. This is the point where we saw upper management begin to disengage from technology-based decisions and defer to the knowledge of others better versed in the tech realm.

So let us imagine it's 2003, and a retailer with multiple locations across the country decides to take a closer look at their inventory systems. They discover that each location has their own system—some still use a paper-based process wherein they manually input data on a paper form into an electronic spreadsheet they send to corporate, and others use a variety of whatever software the general manager decided on.

Obviously, this is going to lead to inefficiencies, as corporate will have to consolidate all of the varied reports coming in, slowing down the forecasting process and leading to logistic problems in which money is wasted by ordering too much of some product, or revenue opportunities are lost by not having enough of a product to meet customer demand.

In this scenario, the product department will want to identify their greatest concerns, assess what options are available to synchronize inventory systems across their locations, and put into place a plan for rolling out the new system and training all the stakeholders impacted by the transformation. The stakeholders in this situation would be not only the inventory leadership at corporate but also the store managers and any of their staff who play an active role in tracking inventory. By creating a single system, it will not only save time for corporate but also will save time (and money) for all their employees, as there will be no need to learn a whole new inventory system if a staff member is moved from one location to another.

While EA 2.0 is certainly more focused and efficiency minded than EA 1.0, the view here was still largely siloed around specific business needs in a segment of the enterprise, rather than taking a holistic view of how a change in one segment will impact and influence other pieces of the enterprise. In the above example, they are only considering how to become more efficient in one process—inventory; they are not looking at the enterprise as a whole to see what else can be optimized.

ENTERPRISE ARCHITECTURE 3.0: 2020 TO PRESENT

Today we are in the era of evolving Enterprise Architecture as business grows increasingly permeable and looking for new ways for industries to integrate with one another. This includes the development of new services and products (like Netflix moving into film production), new partnerships between businesses (like DoorDash providing delivery for restaurants that have never had their own delivery service), or even the acquisition of businesses that cross over into a new industry that impacts the entire structure and business plan of the enterprise (like Amazon acquiring Whole Foods).

Now the development of EA systems and the corresponding interest in it have largely been shaped like a roller coaster, in which the peaks follow a financial crisis. The current era of Enterprise Architecture can be marked as a result of the 2008 recession. Between the financial crises of the dot-com burst and the housing market crash, interest in EA waned, even though the interest in digital technologies and innovation continued to rise. In other words, enterprises generally moved toward a mindset of technology implementation based more on whatever the "new, shiny" thing happened to be at the time.

From 2000 to 2008, people were developing systems left and right, and everyone was jumping on the "digital bandwagon" as digital transformation and tech buzzwords flew around. By this point, we reached a stage at which businesses realized they had to be tech savvy. No business could say, "We don't know tech," and expect to grow—or survive. In fact, this stage could be defined as business and technology becoming one with each other.

But the Great Recession sparked a renewed interest in EA and creating corporate strategy around implementing changes, technological or otherwise. Gone were the assumptions that a business could "wing it" where integrating tech in their business plans was concerned. Rather than relying on trial and error, enterprises became more aware of the need for a holistic and systematic method of decision making and implementation, in which stakeholder concerns would be at the forefront, while potential risks could be mitigated.

In fact, let's go back a minute to discuss further the acquisition of Whole Foods by Amazon. In its relatively short history, Amazon has evolved from their vision to be the largest online bookstore to expanding into a vast marketplace of goods but also expanding into new industries like publishing with its Kindle platform. While that particular expansion was still reasonably aligned with their online bookstore, the move into the grocery business was an enormous transformation—and one that definitely raised eyebrows in the public.

Not only would this impact their mission statement and vision as a company but also their supply chains and certainly HR, as they would be incorporating existing locations and personnel. Making this a smooth process would require more than just a couple of handshakes and financial transactions; it would need an overhaul of the whole business design to increase revenue without losing productivity or efficiency.

While most of the world only sees the results in the stock market or the headlines, an Enterprise Architect can see the intricacies and layers of interconnected decisions that need to be made to impact and optimize all four architecture domains within Amazon: Business, Data, Application, and Technology.

As the world rebounds from the 2020 pandemic, I can imagine we will see a similar trend in which businesses will look more seriously at Enterprise Architecture and how a full-fledged EA plan can help them improve every aspect of their business to adapt to the "new normal" of a postpandemic economy. As enterprises look to adapt, they will need Enterprise Architects to help them create blueprints for optimal business performance.

Common Misconceptions

The first problem I see when it comes to business and technology is a fundamental misunderstanding of what an Enterprise Architect does. Too often, the role is seen as only another IT professional, and because a business already has an IT team, whether internal or external, they fail to see the purpose in hiring an Enterprise Architect or EA firm.

While an IT professional may be very knowledgeable about the latest tech and how to use it or may be well versed on the enterprise's IT infrastructure and needs, that does not mean they possess a full grasp of the mission, needs, and long-term goals of the business. In contrast, an Enterprise Architect's role is to understand all the pieces—IT and business—to find the best path forward.

Another major misconception I see concerns the various methodologies that enterprises turn to when they want to create an EA strategy and implement changes. Two common methodologies are the "waterfall method," which was common in the '90s, and the "Agile method."

> An Enterprise Architect's role is to understand all the pieces—IT and business—to find the best path forward.

If you're unfamiliar with these, the "waterfall method" is where an organization makes decisions one step after another, wherein the outputs of each stage determine the inputs for each successive phase, as follows:

- Gathering of the system requirements

- Analysis of the requirements

- Design of the solution

- Implementation of the solution

- User acceptance testing (UAT)

- Operational rollout

Meanwhile, the "Agile method" is where projects (also called "implementations" or "implementation projects") get broken down into smaller, more manageable chunks to speed up the process of execution. This method has become increasingly popular since the early 2000s, as it is more focused on innovation, and we will discuss it in more detail later in chapter 9. Enterprises often employ this method when they are revising their EA in terms of globalization and digitalization and remaining competitive in a changing market.

While both have their advantages and their places, it can be all too easy for an enterprise to get stuck on these methods—or others—and try to apply the same one in every situation because they are most comfortable with it, rather than looking at how different situations may require different methodologies—or even a combination of methods. Just because something worked in the past does not mean it will work now. After all, I'm sure we are all grateful for advances in medicine that make it possible for us to treat old diseases in new ways. In the same spirit, it takes a discerning and skilled Enterprise Architect to know how best to combine and adapt methods for a specific enterprise's needs.

Conclusion

As we dig deeper into the specific architecture frameworks in the next chapters, it's important to keep this history in mind. We will continue to return to the example of Southeast Regional Bank as we discuss these concepts to help you have a better picture of how Enterprise Architects help businesses. While not every situation will be as complicated as theirs, their process provides plenty of practical examples for us to learn from.

While you do not need to become an Enterprise Architect yourself, I hope that a rudimentary understanding of EA will serve you in the long run as you make decisions that will impact you, your organization, and those that you are hoping to serve. With that, it's time to introduce you to some of the key Enterprise Architecture frameworks that others have used to help them adapt to changing markets, improve their operations, and remain competitive.

CHAPTER TAKEAWAYS

▶ The goal of Enterprise Architecture (EA) is to create a blueprint that will align an enterprise's business strategy to their operations, including their long-term goals and tech needs, providing insight into their current state and their desired state, and optimize the quality of the enterprise's solutions.

▶ EA has evolved from technology driven (EA 1.0) to strategic driven (EA 3.0), with the greatest adoption and interest of EA occurring in the aftermath of a financial upheaval.

▶ When describing a particular architecture as "mature" or "not mature," it has nothing to do with how long the framework has existed but with how completely it addresses the four architecture domains:

1. Business

2. Data

3. Applications

4. Technology

▶ A Strategy Architecture Roadmap is developed by looking at the needs identified across three levels, from "big picture" goals to specific projects and initiatives:

1. Strategy Architecture

2. Segment Architecture

3. Capability Architecture

▶ More of a piece of advice than anything else: No matter what industry you are in or specific service you provide, I believe the history of Enterprise Architecture shows that you should not wait for a crisis to look at your own EA but that it should be a continuous conversation to look at how to best optimize your enterprise.

▶ Finally, it's important to remember that a successful EA plan is not so much about a specific method as it is about having a knowledgeable Enterprise Architect who can craft a holistic process and method customized to your enterprise because they have a clear understanding of your goals and needs.

CHAPTER 2

ENTERPRISE ARCHITECTURE FRAMEWORKS

If you have ever passed by a construction zone, you may have noticed that after the foundation is laid, the next step is to construct the framing. If it is a residential structure like a house or an apartment building, the framing will probably be wood. If it is a commercial property, then it may have steel framing. Regardless of the end design or purpose of the building, the frame is what will help it take shape and determine the strength of the building.

So now that you have a foundation laid for understanding the development and key concepts of Enterprise Architecture, it's time for us to raise the framing by taking a look at the various frameworks that can be used to help organizations bring shape to their EA. While different frameworks have different strengths and challenges to them, they all serve the same general purpose to strengthen the enterprise and help it achieve its long-term goals.

A good working definition of an EA framework is that it "describe[s] the underlying infrastructure, thus providing the groundwork for the hardware, software, and networks to work together."[1] But it also lays out a methodical, repeatable, and systematic view of the specific needs of the enterprise.

So let's first return to our friends at Southeast Regional Bank. They knew that they were in desperate need of an Enterprise Architecture strategy, and they knew what their end goals were. With EA though, especially when looking at an organization with so many complicated layers, there is no simple Step 1, Step 2 process like following a recipe.

That doesn't mean the process is without direction, however. The framework not only helps define the direction for the process, but it also ensures that the steps taken move in the direction of the defined goals. Too often, without a structured framework, an enterprise can get lost in the weeds, distracted by new tech, and find themselves in a cycle of indecision or indirection.

In fact, selecting the correct framework can be something of an art for the Enterprise Architect. They must have both a deep knowledge of the organization's needs *and* the various available frameworks to select the right one that will not only achieve the desired end state but will also simplify the process without sacrificing thoroughness. Enterprise Architecture can prove challenging enough, so there is no need to make it more difficult than necessary!

Before we discuss in more detail the specific frameworks, there are a few key elements to understand about them.

---

1   Lise Urbaczewski, "A Comparison of Enterprise Architecture Frameworks," *Eastern Michigan University: Issues in Information Systems* 7, no. 2 (2006): 18.

Framework Element One: Understanding the Enterprise

First, it is the role of the Enterprise Architect to understand the organization's context for conducting the EA process and understand their industry in order to suggest the correct framework—or a combination of multiple frameworks more often than not.

For example, in the case of Southeast Regional Bank, it was apparent to me that they needed to implement two distinct frameworks: one for their overall business needs to help them organize all the complicated components and bring synchronicity to their siloed business units and disparate IT capabilities, and another framework tailored more to their industry needs as a provider of financial services.

A skilled Enterprise Architect knows how to not only select the correct framework but also knows how to tailor and customize it to the enterprise's specific needs. In my experience, an enterprise is already inclined toward a specific framework about half of the time, but it is important for the architect to be able to make recommendations based on a full understanding of the enterprise.

A skilled Enterprise Architect knows how to not only select the correct framework but also knows how to tailor and customize it.

Framework Element Two: Customization

Second, it's important for anyone beginning an EA process to know that they are generally designed to be customizable to address the specific enterprise's pain points. A standard of proven EA frameworks is that they are generic enough to be applied across not only various enterprises but also various industries.

In general, most frameworks are designed to be business oriented—that is, centered upon the business's overall needs. There are some that are more technology oriented, but regardless, they remain customizable.

With the case of Southeast Regional Bank, the view was to tailor the chosen framework to help them meet their needs as a provider of financial services. This meant we could essentially "skip" over some aspects of the framework and devote our time and energy to those areas that were more important from a banking perspective. One misconception of EA is that you must address every piece of the chosen framework to the enterprise. But when you truly understand the enterprise's needs and goals, it empowers you to be more efficient by only addressing the necessary components without wasting time or resources on aspects that simply do not apply to that enterprise's situation.

Framework Element Three: Building Blocks

Different frameworks are designed to meet the needs of different sets of stakeholders and varying issues, or "building blocks" as we refer to them. These blocks are intended to represent the standards, methods, tools, and even common vocabulary that will create clear communication throughout the process and implementation of those tools.

It's also these building blocks that help the Enterprise Architect customize the EA and keep track of the various inputs and outputs of each stage of the EA design. While not every framework has a clearly defined process, they all have well-defined building blocks.

We will discuss later what the building blocks looked like for Southeast Regional Bank, but suffice it to say for now that Architecture Building Blocks (ABBs) ultimately exist to define and guide the Solution Building Blocks (SBBs) that will be developed by the architecture. Throughout the process, you may find that different building blocks play a role in multiple levels of the enterprise, making them more valuable, as they can be reused.

Meet the Frameworks

The history of EA has seen the development of a number of commonly known and utilized frameworks. However, we will not be discussing these in chronological order but rather in terms of how popular they are. While there may be some differing views on this within my industry, I believe it to be accurate based on my own experience.

Also, please note that this is not an exhaustive list. In the next chapter, we will introduce some industry-specific reference frameworks, but here we will focus on industry-neutral frameworks so that you can have at least some familiarity with the options available to you.

TOGAF®

The Open Group Architecture Framework (TOGAF®), which was developed by the Open Group, has become the industry standard since its inception in 1995 during the era of Enterprise Architecture 1.0. As the most popular framework, it has provided a proven methodology for some of the world's leading companies, including the likes of IBM, Intel, Philips, and Huawei. In fact, TOGAF® represents 60–80 percent of the market share in terms of how often it is utilized compared to other frameworks.

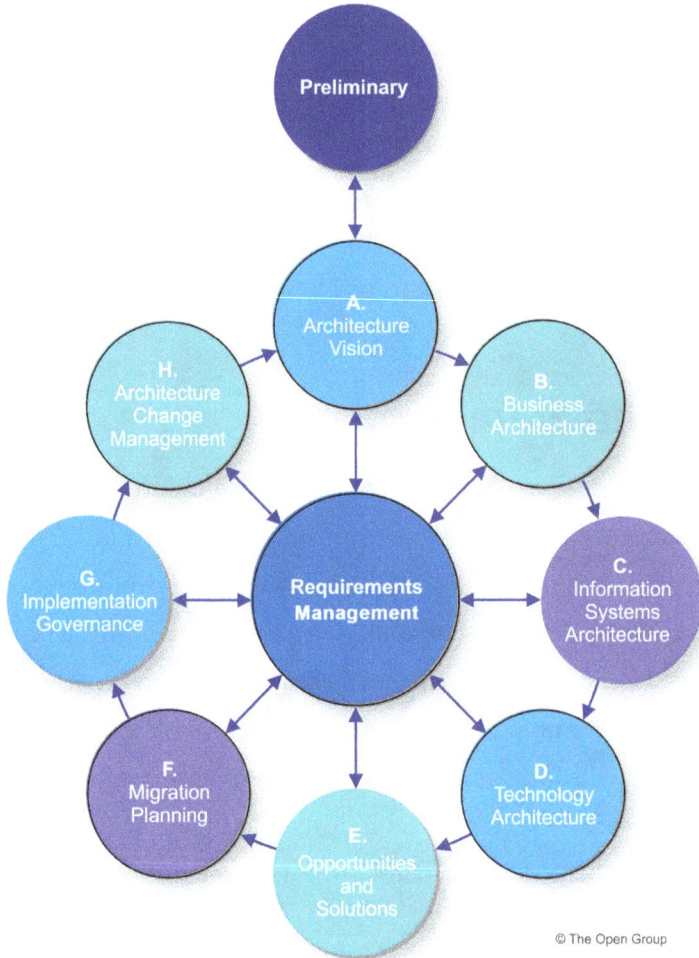

© The Open Group

I often encourage those pursuing a career in Enterprise Architecture to get certified in TOGAF® because of the breadth of its process and adaptability. As a framework, it has a very mature structure, meaning that it addresses all four architecture domains of business, application, data, and technology. In chapter 4, I will provide a more detailed description of its specific components and process. For now, it's enough to say that its breadth and thoroughness is exactly why it is so popular.

Strengths:

- Consists of a clearly defined process that is adaptable and repeatable.
- Can be combined with any other framework as needed.
- Business oriented rather than technology oriented.
- Covers all four domain architectures.

Challenges:

- Specifications of the framework are massive, so it is easy for one to get lost in it.
- Not as user friendly as some of the other less complicated frameworks.

Some clarifying thoughts on these challenges: One of the great misconceptions I see about TOGAF® is that oftentimes a leader thinks they must use every component of the framework for their enterprise and forget that it can be tailored. TOGAF® is designed to be thorough so that it can be applied across a large variety of situations, but that doesn't mean every step in it applies to every enterprise. Therefore, as I mentioned before, there may be components of the process that do not apply and can be skipped over.

In terms of user friendliness, TOGAF® is moderately user friendly because it can be understood fairly easily on a high level, but in terms of execution, it can become complicated. However, that is also part of the importance for an enterprise to have a TOGAF®-certified Enterprise Architect providing guidance throughout the process to ensure that no one gets lost along the way and that all bases are covered.

	STRATEGISTS	EXECUTIVE LEADERS	ARCHITECTS	ENGINEERS	TECHNICIANS	WORKERS	
WHY	Motivation Identification	Motivation Definition	Motivation Representation	Motivation Specification	Motivation Configuration	Motivation Instantiation	MOTIVATION
WHEN	Timing Identification	Timing Definition	Timing Representation	Timing Specification	Timing Configuration	Timing Instantiation	TIMING
WHO	Organization Identification	Organization Definition	Organization Representation	Organization Specification	Organization Configuration	Organization Instantiation	ORGANIZATION
WHERE	Network Identification	Network Definition	Network Representation	Network Specification	Network Configuration	Network Instantiation	NETWORK
HOW	Process Identification	Process Definition	Process Representation	Process Specification	Process Configuration	Process Instantiation	PROCESS
WHAT	Inventory Indentification	Inventory Definition	Inventory Representation	Inventory Specification	Inventory Configuration	Inventory Instantiation	INVENTORY
	SCOPE	BUSINESS	SYSTEM	TECHNOLOGY	COMPONENT	OPERATIONS	

ZACHMAN

As the creator of the first EA framework, Zachman is often referred to as "the father of Enterprise Architecture." It was first developed in 1987 by John Zachman as business and technology began to intersect more, and it currently exists in version 3.0. Zachman noticed how IT decisions were being made and integrated into business on an ad hoc basis with little planning or strategy. Seeing the problems that could lead to, he sought to find a more analytical method to identify an enterprise's target architecture, or "future state," for better implementing IT solutions.

As seen in the previous graphic, Zachman is a two-dimensional six-by-six matrix. The upper horizontal row is known as "Interrogatives," asking the classic questions of "What, How, Where, Who, When, and Why?" and intended to help the enterprise ask the right questions in a strategic manner.

Meanwhile, the left-side vertical row of "Perspectives" is made up of various dimensions that need to be considered in light of the "Interrogatives." Each successive row is driven by the row above it, as follows:

- The first row considers the "Scope" of the enterprise, developed by the strategist(s).

- The second row looks at the "Business" that was determined by the Scope and identified by the executive leaders.

- The third row gives you the "Systems" for the Business, as determined by the architect(s).

- The fourth row looks at the "Technology," the infrastructure needed to build the Systems, as identified by the engineers.

- The fifth row looks at the "Components" of the Technology and Business, determined by the technicians.

- And finally, the sixth row considers the "Operations"—that is, how all of the above dimensions will be carried out by the workers.

Deriving from the basis of Greek philosophy, the purpose of the schema is to overlay and intersect each Interrogative with each Perspective of the enterprise to identify and describe the needs to be addressed by the architecture. As such, Zachman is an ontology rather than a methodology, meaning it provides a comprehensive view of the necessary architecture, but it does not provide a step-by-step process for executing it. Instead, the specific process of carrying it out must be determined by the enterprise or Enterprise Architect.

Strengths:

- Can fit any enterprise
- Easy to understand and use

Challenges:

- Lacks a complete process to collect the information
- Unclear on order of steps, how to implement transformations

Zachman is still a very popular framework in use, thanks to its long presence in the EA industry and because of its adaptability and high level of user friendliness. For a simpler enterprise, it can sometimes prove more efficient than TOGAF®, though elements of TOGAF® can certainly be considered to help address the lack of a clear process to follow.

ENTERPRISE ARCHITECTURE PLANNING (EAP)

Steven Spewak developed the Enterprise Architecture Planning (EAP) framework in 1992. Spewak sought to expand upon Zachman's framework by developing a methodology. While it is also business oriented, EAP approaches the EA process from a data-centric view, in which the data is driven by the business mission rather than by the applications.

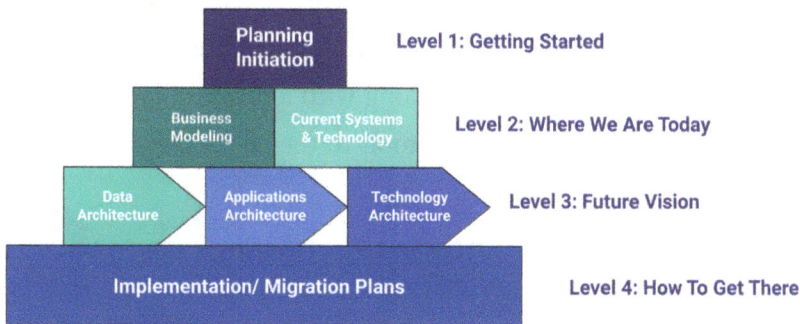

The EAP model is composed of four layers:

Level 1, "Getting Started," involves the high-level management personnel that need to make the initial decisions regarding the EA process, including the "buy-in" to the process, how they will resource and support the process, what tools will be used to execute the plan, and who needs to be involved.

Level 2, "Where We Are Today," determines the baseline of the enterprise, the starting point of what the current architecture looks like. It typically consists of (1) Business Process Modeling, a model that will compile the knowledge of business functions and information used in supporting and conducting the business processes, and (2) Current Systems and Technology, an identification of the current applications and technology platforms in use. This can help the enterprise notice any deficiencies or pain points that may need to be addressed.

Level 3, "Where We Want To Be," defines the vision for the domains of Data, Applications, and Technology by setting a target architecture to be achieved through transformation. Here the enterprise looks at how those deficiencies and pain points in Level 2 will be fulfilled.

Level 4, "How We Get There," consists of an Implementation Plan and Migration Plan through a specified sequence and schedule of changes being made to the various architectures. This typically includes a cost/benefits analysis along with a detailed and clear path for migration from the old set of tools to the new set.

Strengths:

- Business mission oriented and addresses all four domains
- Very adaptable and user friendly
- Provides a methodology

Challenges:

- Outdated, has not been improved upon since its development
- Considered unsuccessful by some in the industry and therefore is not very popular

A further note on these challenges: While EAP appears on paper to be an improvement upon Zachman by defining a process, it has not always proved so in its execution. For that reason, Zachman remains somewhat popular, while EAP has fallen by the wayside and has not been revisited seriously due to lacking a track record of success. Still, EAP is worth knowing about, as it was the first step in advancing EA in the direction of a repeatable and adaptable method.

GARTNER

This framework was developed as the result of Gartner, Inc. acquiring Meta Group in 2005. Meta Group had already developed a good EA process before the acquisition, so Gartner combined this with their EA taxonomy they had been developing as part of their IT consulting services. Now, with both the taxonomy and methodology, they hoped to have a complete framework that they could put into practice with their business model.

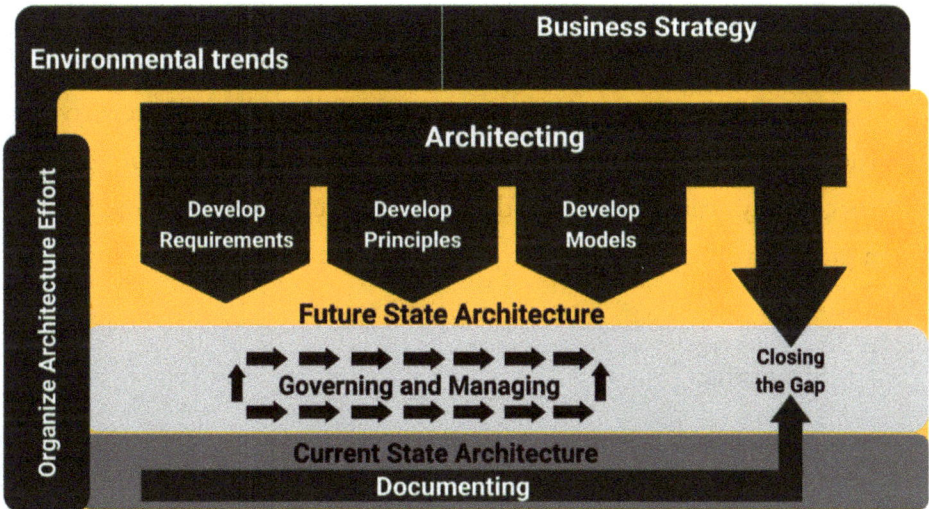

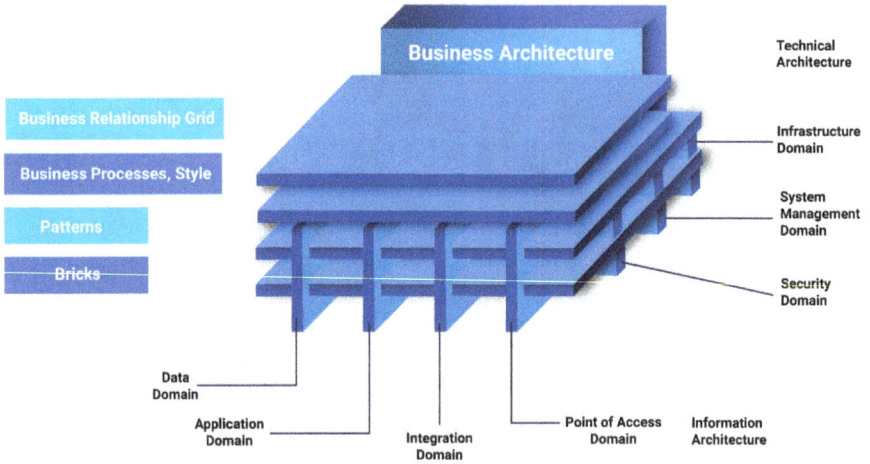

However, during the merger, many of the Meta Group personnel who were experts in their EA process did not join with Gartner and left to either join other companies or strike out on their own. Therefore, Gartner did not acquire the expertise or the full intellectual property they had expected, so to my knowledge, their framework has not been successfully utilized outside of their own services. Instead, it's become a proprietary framework to serve the EA needs of their clients.

Strengths:

- Business oriented
- Includes methodology

Challenges:

- Proprietary framework, not accessible to everyone

It is a fair question to ask me why I even mention the Gartner framework when it is not accessible to other enterprises, but I mention it because it is indicative of the evolution of the mindset that a successful EA should have not only a taxonomy like Zachman but also a methodology. And even more important than that, I think it is proof that successful application of a framework requires expertise to guide the process.

For those who decide to become a Gartner client and engage with their EA tools, there can be other benefits, including access to their other business services, such as auditing and risk assessment, HR services, and even marketing and communications functions. Beyond that, Gartner has services and processes customized by industry for those who decide to become clients.

> Successful application of a framework requires expertise to guide the process.

INTEGRATED ARCHITECTURE FRAMEWORK (IAF)

The final framework we'll discuss here is the Integrated Architecture Framework that was developed by Capgemini during the '90s and first released in 1996. It was originally based on both the Zachman and the EAP frameworks and is currently in its sixth version. Capgemini's view in the architecture was to provide a holistic view across business, information, systems, and technology. They did not want to simply design IT systems but to create a method to deliver business change that could be supported and enabled by IT.

Integrated Architecture Framework

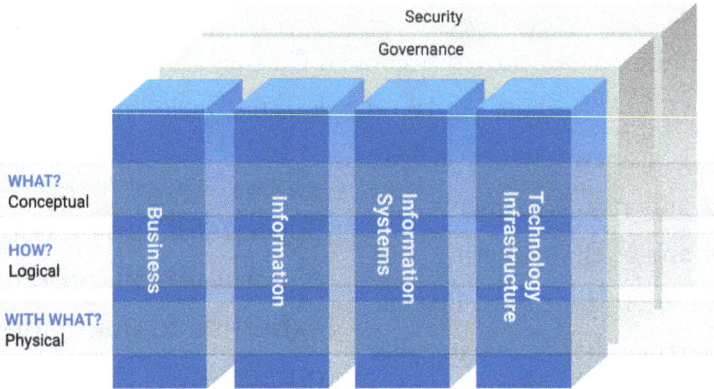

Like Gartner, however, IAF is a proprietary framework, so one must be a client to benefit from it. Generally speaking, though, the IAF process follows six main stages:

- Vision: What do we want the architecture to achieve?

- Strategy: How do we want to achieve it?

- Design: What solution architecture is needed? Whom will it serve?

- Deliver: How, When, and to Whom do we deliver the solution architecture?

- Deploy: Execute the implementation of new systems and applications.

- Retire: Discontinue the use of old systems and applications no longer required.

Strengths:

- Holistic; considers all four domains
- Provides methodology

Challenges:

- Not user friendly due to being a proprietary framework

Again, IAF shows the trend in EA to take a holistic view of the business by putting the business needs first and implementing a defined process. Like with Gartner, those who decide to enlist Capgemini's services to utilize IAF in their EA transformation can also have access to their other services, which include areas like AI, cybersecurity services, and cloud services implementation.

Conclusion

Now in the case of Southeast Regional Bank, the option was pretty clear which framework would be relied upon, as they needed not only a holistic overhaul of their business needs but a clear and proven process. While a framework like Zachman's would have helped them identify what they needed to accomplish, they would not have known where to even begin to address the complicated layers of transformations they hoped to make.

Of the frameworks presented here, it was decided that TOGAF® was the most suitable for their situation due to its adaptability—and would also allow further tailoring with an industry-specific framework like what we will discuss in chapter 3. Certainly, there is a time and place for these other frameworks, which is why I think you should know about all of them. At the end of the day, the important thing is to select a framework that matches your enterprise's needs and will have the full commitment of the stakeholders.

Armed with an understanding of the available EA frameworks and the needs they address, you and your Enterprise Architect can make a more informed decision on what will best suit your needs. The unifying advantage of these frameworks, though, is their capacity to meet the needs of enterprises across industries.

Still, there are occasions in which you must think about your industry first and how the framework can help you adapt to changes in the market, remain competitive, and be prepared for the future based on industry trends. It is in those instances that industry-specific reference frameworks can be harnessed to achieve the full potential of your EA plan.

CHAPTER TAKEAWAYS

▶ Zachman's was the first EA framework developed in the late '80s and is still in use today. It provided an easy-to-use taxonomy for identifying enterprise needs but no process.

▶ TOGAF® is the most popular EA framework, thanks to its adaptability to any enterprise situation and having both a taxonomy and methodology.

▶ Frameworks may be combined or adapted to meet a specific enterprise's needs.

▶ The most successful frameworks are business oriented rather than technology oriented. In other words, the technology solutions are not central to the strategy but rather support the business strategy.

▶ As helpful as it is to have a process and follow it, it's important to keep in mind that you don't have to utilize every single piece of the process. Instead, you should focus on the pieces that are specific to your organization and implement those with the guidance of an Enterprise Architect knowledgeable in both the enterprise's needs and the framework to be used.

CHAPTER 3

REFERENCE ARCHITECTURES

A simple problem often requires a simple solution. Likewise, a complex problem requires a more complex solution. Such was the case with Southeast Regional Bank as we began the EA process with them. And because their situation had so many layers, it required a layered approach.

As I mentioned in the last chapter, it can be easy for a business leader new to the EA process to look at their selected framework and fall into the trap of following every step and forcing solutions where perhaps no solution was truly required. As the saying goes, popularized by businessman Bert Lance: "If it ain't broke, don't fix it."

Yet another pitfall that sometimes occurs with those new to EA is forgetting that the process needs to be adapted not only to the organization but potentially to the industry they exist within. Ignoring the industry—its market trends, competition, standards, and regulations—could lead to an oversight that hurts the enterprise's Agility over the long term.

Therefore, sometimes it is necessary to adapt the EA framework with a reference architecture that has been designed for a specific purpose or industry. With Southeast Regional Bank, then, this meant not only applying the TOGAF® framework but also looking in the banking sector and applying a methodology developed specifically with the financial services industry in mind.

Ignoring the industry—its market trends, competition, standards, and regulations—could lead to an oversight that hurts the enterprise's Agility over the long term.

While not every industry has a specific reference architecture, there have been a number of frameworks developed for major industries throughout the course of the past few decades. As we did in the last chapter, we will look at the basics of what each reference architecture is designed for, its advantages, and its potential challenges.

Telecom Industry: Frameworx

Developed by the TeleManagement Forum (TM Forum), Frameworx was initially released in 2000 as an adaptable toolkit that has become widely utilized across the telecom industry. TM Forum is an international alliance of over eight hundred telecommunications companies that requires a paid membership to benefit from their resources, including Frameworx, which is designed to benefit any enterprise within the telecom space, including such major players as AT&T, Verizon, and Nippon. Like many EA processes, the goal of Frameworx is to help "improve agility in IT and operations, resulting in increased margins, lower costs and optimal customer experience."[2]

---

2   "Code + Frameworks," TM Forum, accessed May 24, 2021, https://www.tmforum.org/frameworx-homepage/.

OPEN DIGITAL FRAMEWORK

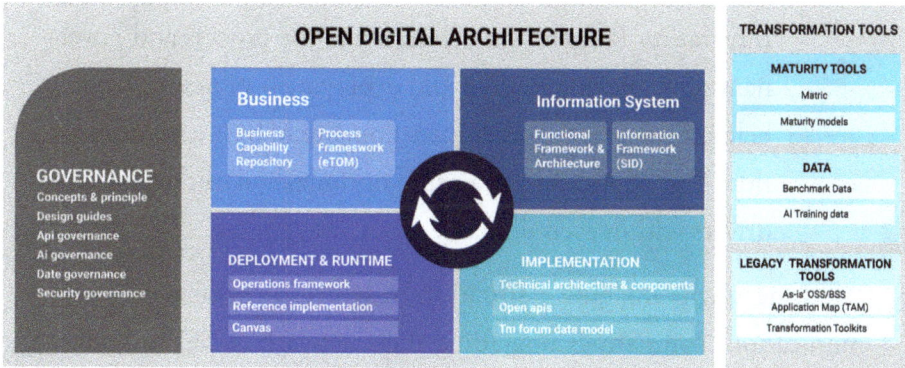

One of the major strengths of Frameworx is that it has been improved over time to include and address all four domains of business, data, application, and technology through four frameworks:

- Business Process Framework: eTOM (enhanced Telecom Operations Map) is an enterprise framework developed for use within the telecommunications industry by providing a set of standards, models, and best practices.

- Data Process Framework: Shared Information/Data model (otherwise known as SID), a model designed to provide standard definitions for all information flowing through the enterprise and also between the service providers and their business partners.

- Application Framework: Telecom Application Map (or TAM) is a model providing a formalized method for grouping together enterprise functions and data into components, considering the role and functionality of the various applications that deliver the OSS (Operations Support System) and BSS (Business Support System) capabilities.

- Technology Framework: Developed as part of the TM Forum Integration Program (or TIP), at the center of Frameworx. The Integration Program model describes the process and governance for implementation and deployment of new solutions, helping connect the other three domains of business, information, and application to ensure optimization and enable the drivers within each domain.

One might imagine a situation in which a regional telecommunications company is upgrading their network to 5G to remain competitive, but this will require a reassessment and reoptimization of their entire business strategy. Assuming that they are already a member of the TM Forum, Frameworx would be the ideal reference architecture for them to pursue when embarking on an EA process. Since it has a proven track record with others in the same space, the leadership team can have confidence that it can be adapted for their needs to help them reach their target architectural design.

Strengths:

- Mature design that considers all four domains
- Fairly user friendly and self-explanatory

Challenges:

- Enterprise must be a member of TM Forum to benefit, which will incur an additional cost

In many cases within the telecom industry, Frameworx may be utilized alone to address the enterprise's needs since it takes a holistic approach. Even so, there may be occasions when it makes sense to combine it with another framework like TOGAF®. One could also make the argument that an enterprise could utilize a framework like Zachman to identify their needs and goals but then apply Frameworx for executing the exact process.

Banking/Financial Services Industry: BIAN

BIAN (Banking Industry Architecture Network) was established in 2008 as a member-owned, nonprofit association and is currently in version 8.0. Like TM Forum for telecom, BIAN requires membership, which includes various benefits, including their reference architecture framework tailored specifically for any enterprise in the banking or financial services sector.

Next to TM Forum, I would classify BIAN as the next most mature model in this list, especially since its implementation process is designed to align with TOGAF®'s ADM. While it addresses multiple domains, it does not do so with equal thoroughness:

- Business Domain: Mostly considers business services, not the full business strategy.

- Applications Domain: Has a pretty mature consideration of web applications, including clearly defined APIs (Application Programming Interfaces) being utilized within the industry.

- Data Domain: While some data is given consideration, mostly in reference to the APIs addressed in the applications domain, it is otherwise a weaker point in the framework.

- Technology: Interoperability of banking solutions is a key component of BIAN; therefore, the technology solutions tend to be heavily considered and addressed.

Enterprise Management and Controlling		Product and Service Enabling	
Business Direction Management	Business Entity Management	Agreement Management	Financial Plan Management
Policy Management	Risk Management	Financial Instrument Management	Investment portfolio Management
Finance Management	Investor Management	Issued Device Management	Money Movement Management
Fraud Management		Order Management	Product Management
		Trade Finance Management	Trust Management
		Payment Management	

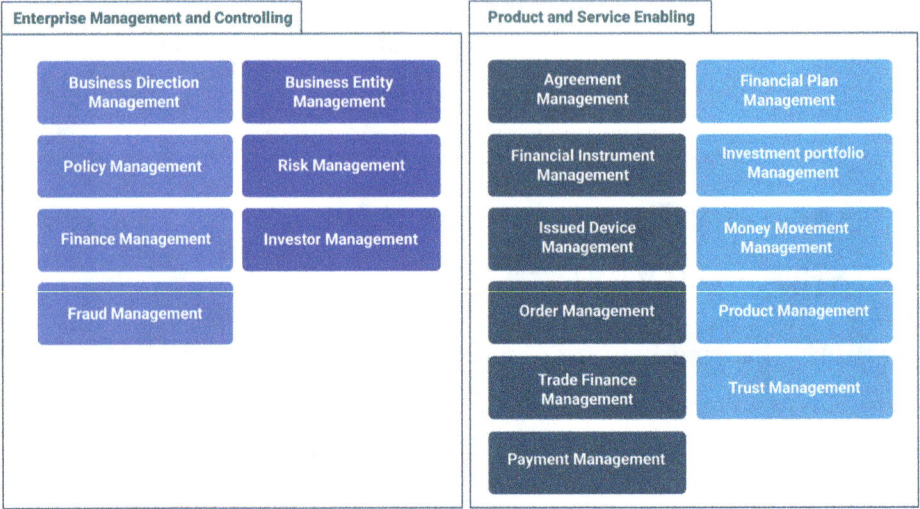

Given its focus on banking applications, BIAN is an ideal framework that can be harnessed by large, layered financial institutions like JPMorgan Chase, Bank of America, credit unions, or even regional banks, such as Southeast Regional Bank. In fact, BIAN is the reference architecture that we combined with TOGAF® to help guide their EA optimization, looking at the trends in the banking space and benefiting from what had already proven successful for others in the industry.

Strengths:

- Decently mature framework that considers at least some aspects of each domain
- Strong focus on applications (APIs)

Challenges:

- Must be a member of BIAN to benefit from it
- Typically needs to be combined with another framework to help address gaps

Enterprise Enabling	Bank Operations	Customer and Sales	Channels
Facility and Equipment Management	Colateral Management	Customer Management	Channel Management
Human Capital Management	Physical Cash Management	Marketing	Partner Management
Information Management		Sale Management	
Vendor & Supplier Management			
Legal Support Management			
Workflow Management			

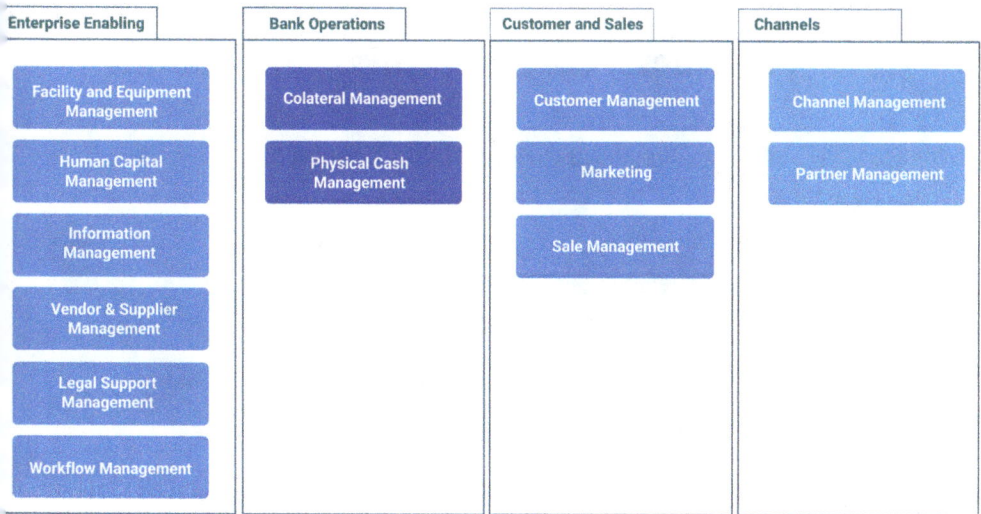

Overall, BIAN is a thorough reference architecture and can certainly help simplify and focus the optimization process for those in the financial services sector. In general, it is fairly user friendly, though the assistance of an experienced Enterprise Architect is strongly recommended to help fill in the gaps in the business and data domains that may be better addressed by another framework like TOGAF®.

Retail Industry: ARTS

The Association for Retail Technology Standards (ARTS) Operational Data Model (ODM) is a twenty-year-old reference framework designed to identify, define, and describe transaction data for those in the retail industry. It was originally developed to address individual store-based retail transactions and then evolved into an architectural model that could support global operations for retail giants, including the likes of Tesco in the UK or Walmart in the United States. In its current version (7.3), it has expanded to help these retailers better track and understand consumer behavior.

Products, Services, Rules, and Tax

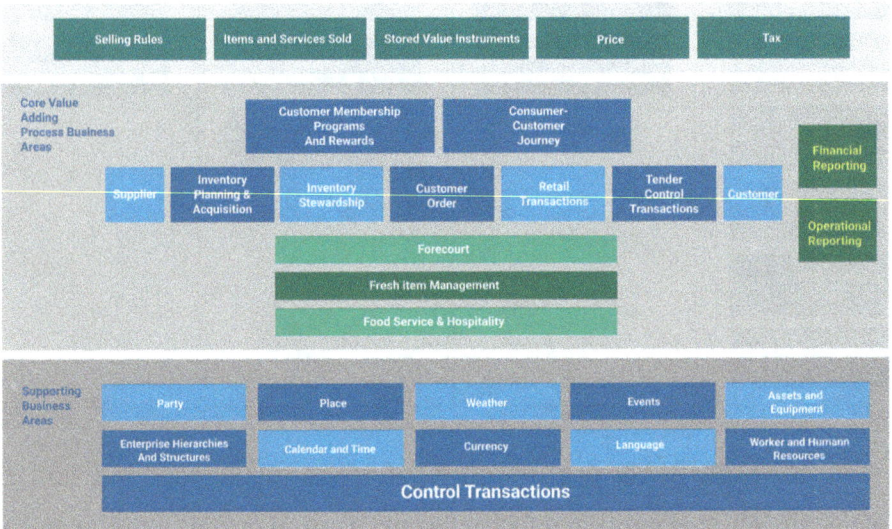

| Selling Rules | Items and Services Sold | Stored Value Instruments | Price | Tax |

Core Value Adding Process Business Areas

Customer Membership Programs And Rewards · Consumer-Customer Journey · Financial Reporting

Supplier · Inventory Planning & Acquisition · Inventory Stewardship · Customer Order · Retail Transactions · Tender Control Transactions · Customer · Operational Reporting

Forecourt

Fresh Item Management

Food Service & Hospitality

Supporting Business Areas

Party · Place · Weather · Events · Assets and Equipment

Enterprise Hierarchies And Structures · Calendar and Time · Currency · Language · Worker and Human Resources

Control Transactions

However, an enterprise does not have to be a global entity to benefit. A retail-based organization of any size can scale the framework for both the size of their enterprise and also in consideration of their long-term goals, such as adding future locations or other expansion.

The data architecture for ARTS is particularly strong as they utilize logical data models within their process, which is broken up into three main layers:

- Products, Services, Rules, and Tax (includes selling rules, pricing, items and services sold, tax, etc.)

- Core Value Adding Process Business Areas (includes customer membership programs and rewards, supplier relations, inventory planning and stewardship, customer orders, transaction controls, etc.)

- Supporting Business Areas (including enterprise hierarchies and structures, calendar and time, currency, location, events, assets and equipment, human resources, etc.)

From these layers, a retailer can identify their baselines in each area along with their target architectures to help identify the solutions needed to bridge those gaps. However, the business domain is not well defined by the process, and in my view, the applications domain feels somewhat lacking. Still, it provides a thorough set of data structures tailored for the retail environment that could be overlooked by a non-industry-specific framework.

For example, imagine a local clothing retailer that is expanding into another town. ARTS can be utilized to help them be more organized in replicating the aspects of their business that are working well for their new location, while simultaneously identifying areas that may require improvement. Perhaps their current supplier for a set of products will not ship in a timely manner to their new location. They will need to either find a new supplier or else optimize their inventory process to accommodate for the longer shipping time, which could possibly impact the cost of items. Or perhaps the new location has a different tax rate from the original location, which will need to be factored into pricing and expenses. An enterprise will want to consider all of these factors as they plan their expansion and growth to ensure they are getting the most out of the investment.

Strengths:

- Very mature approach for the data domain
- Very adaptable and scalable for retail organizations of any size

Challenges:

- Not as mature in design as other reference frameworks
- Not as user friendly since it does not consider all domains

An enterprise will want to consider all of these factors as they plan their expansion and growth to ensure they are getting the most out of the investment.

Like BIAN, I believe ARTS is best applied when combined with a more mature architecture framework that will address some of the other domains such as business and technology. Still, for those in the retail industry, it can prove to be a thorough and relatively simple framework to apply and help identify areas of improvement.

Defense Industry: DoDAF

DoDAF (Department of Defense Architecture Framework) is a date-centric reference architecture that was developed by the US Department of Defense along with help from Carnegie Mellon. It was originally created following the passage of the Clinger-Cohen Act in 1996, which mandated IT architecture across government organizations, including the Department of Defense. Thanks to having a good budget for its development, DoDAF is a rather robust framework that addresses all four domains.

The original version of the DoD's framework was known as the C4ISR Architecture Framework (Command, Control, Computers, and Communication of Intelligence, Surveillance and Reconnaissance), integrating a reference model called TAFIM (Technology Architecture Framework help from Carnegie Mellon.

for Information Management) that had been initiated in the mid-'80s. From there, it evolved into DoDAF version 1.0, version 1.5, and currently version 2.0.

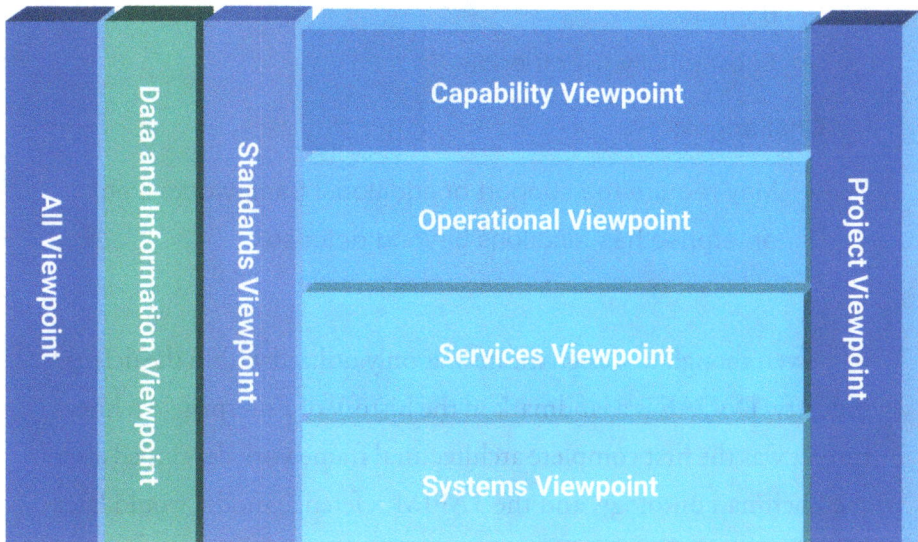

			Capability Viewpoint	
All Viewpoint	Data and Information Viewpoint	Standards Viewpoint	Operational Viewpoint	Project Viewpoint
			Services Viewpoint	
			Systems Viewpoint	

While it was originally created by and for the Department of Defense, it is user friendly enough that it can be adapted and applied for any other defense enterprise, including for-profit businesses like Lockheed Martin, Raytheon, or Boeing Defense, Space & Security. In fact, the UK utilizes a similar framework known as MODAF (Ministry of Defence Architecture Framework). Likewise, it could conceivably be used as a starting point by other national governments desiring to optimize their defense departments.

For example, you might imagine a nation that has an army and navy but decides to build an air force. They could utilize DoDAF as a means to establish a holistic architecture for how their air force will function, from its business structures, data collection capabilities, and the necessary applications and technology to execute their mission.

Strengths:

- Very mature architectural design that covers all four domains
- Substantially user friendly

Challenges:

- May require the support of additional frameworks if an enterprise has functions beyond defense

Even though its design means it is only utilized within the defense industry, DoDAF is a landmark in the history of Enterprise Architecture. It was the first complete architectural framework developed after the Zachman ontology, and the TAFIM reference model would later help give rise to TOGAF®.

Health Industry: HL7

Founded in 1987, Health Level Seven International (HL7) is a nonprofit organization that develops standards and solutions for empowering interoperability of global health data. Because it defines a set of international standards, it is most often used for data being transferred and shared between healthcare providers, especially in terms of bridging gaps between IT applications.

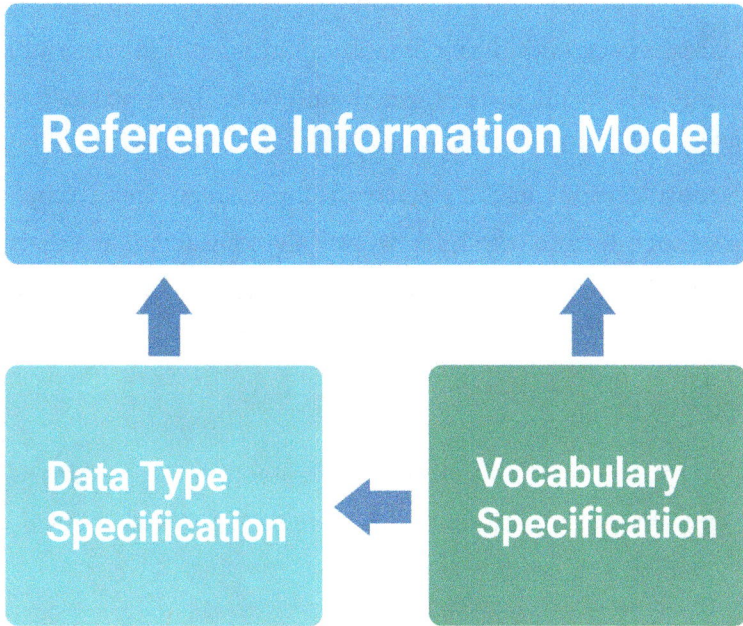

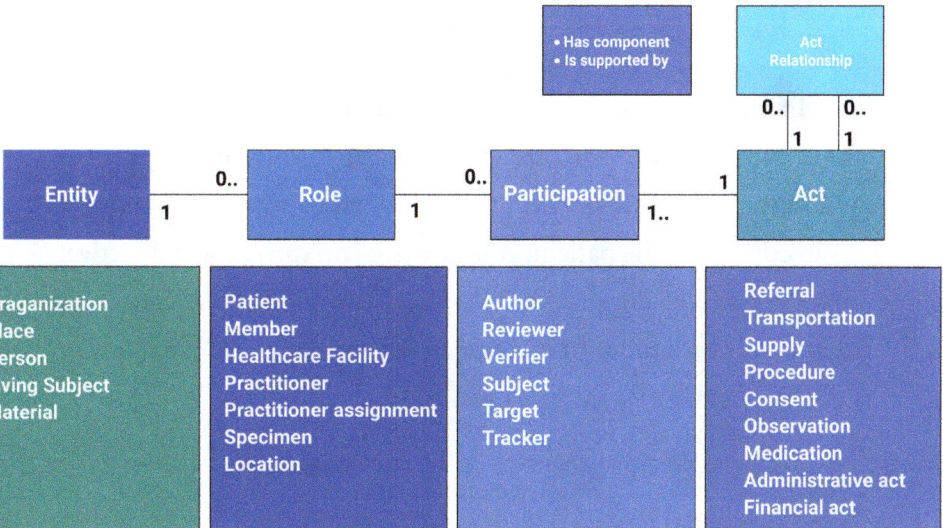

Its creation was a result not only of the necessity for messaging standards between healthcare organizations but also the necessity for standards of how those messages should flow. Their primary focus is on the application and technology architectures, but they do not have considerations in the framework for business architecture. As for data architecture, the framework only considers it in regard to the messaging standards, so it is not as mature as other frameworks.

Strengths:

- Thorough with applications Architecture Capabilities
- User friendly for its purposes since it provides international standards and solutions

Challenges:

- Not a mature framework overall, which would need to be combined with other frameworks to fill in the gaps

In its current version (3.0), the framework provides a helpful industry perspective for meeting the needs of healthcare providers and how they exchange medical records, especially in terms of how it directly affects the patient. A healthcare enterprise could effectively apply it when looking at their applications architecture but would need to rely on a more fully realized framework like TOGAF® for full implementation of an EA process.

Insurance Industry: ACORD

According to their website, "The Association for Cooperative Operations Research and Development (ACORD) Reference Architecture provides an Enterprise Architecture framework for the insurance industry. It consists of business processes, product models, development frameworks, information models, data models, and capability models which help organizations to run, develop, modify, and maintain various insurance industry applications."[3] The framework can be utilized and subscribed to, whether or not one has an ACORD membership, and it is made up of seven components:

- Business Glossary: This is a standard glossary of nontechnical definitions and descriptions of insurance terminology, concepts, and references that will be utilized throughout the other components of the framework.

- Information Model: A conceptual and comprehensive representation of the various data elements, providing a broad view of the relationships between various insurance concepts, linking together all the standards of the ACORD framework.

- Data Model: Generated from the information model, the data model exists to be utilized in database implementation and can be used for designing physical data models and data warehouses, and it also provides best practices for the physical implementation of the data.

- Capability Model: This defines a baseline for the tasks happening across the value chain, presenting those activities in a functional decomposition that can be used in merger and divestiture evaluations, process engineering, and analysis of the business operations.

- Component Model: Contains the information and properties that are required for specific business capabilities making up the insurance business processes, bridging the business

---

3   "Acord Reference Architecture," Acord.org, accessed May 25, 2021, https://www.acord.org/standards-architecture/reference-architecture.

concepts in the capability model and the data concepts in the information model.

- Process Model: Defines a set of reference processes for the insurance industry that are aligned to the capability model to provide a workflow-oriented implementation of the processes and ACORD messages, resulting in a cohesive model adapted for the enterprise's needs.

- Product Framework: This final model enables the users to easily, quickly, and precisely represent the full set of insurance products in a way that will be useful to all levels of the enterprise and is complemented by the ACORD Product Schema.

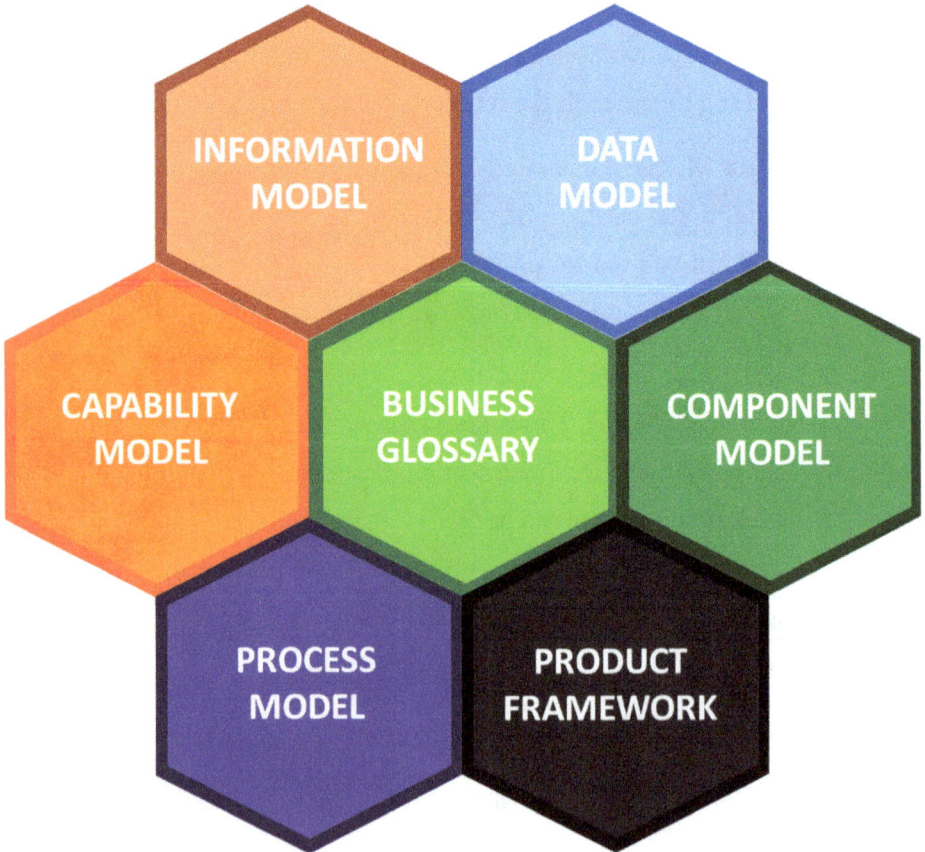

Overall, ACORD is a fairly mature and user-friendly framework and continues to be improved, especially in the domain of business architecture, so it is fair to hope it will continue to be used and improved over time as the industry undergoes more transformations. It is most often used by enterprises in the medical insurance field, but it could be utilized with others in insurance, such as auto, home, or life insurance.

Strengths:

- Overall mature framework when compared to other industry reference frameworks
- Has improved over time, especially in the business architecture domain

Challenges:

- Sometimes ignored by Enterprise Architects in favor of other standards

As a reference framework, I find ACORD to be one of the most holistic. However, it can sometimes be dismissed by Enterprise Architects because they assume that if they are going to use a fully mature process, then they should just use TOGAF® instead. In its defense, though, there can be a real advantage to an enterprise utilizing something that has already been proven successful in its own field and benefiting from those results.

> There can be a real advantage to an enterprise utilizing something that has already been proven successful in its own field.

Federal Government: FEAF

The Federal Enterprise Architecture Framework was developed by the US Office of Management and Budget and first published by the Federal CIO Council in 1999 to provide a common approach in how federal-level government organizations could integrate strategy, business, and technology management.

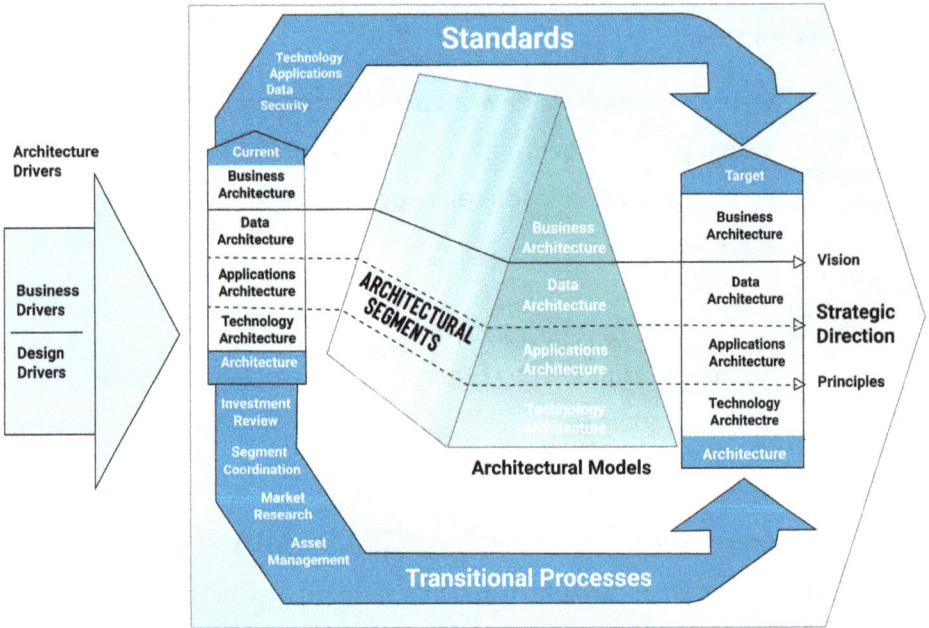

Like DoDAF, its creation can point back to the Clinger-Cohen Act of 1996, when Enterprise Architecture was recognized as a best practice for federal agencies. Now in its second version, FEAF is a very mature framework composed of six strong reference models:

- Performance Reference Model (PRM): This model facilitates the allocation of resources based on the comparative determinations of which programs and organizations show the most efficiency and effectiveness, enabling the agency to be more strategic in their business management.

- Business Reference Model (BRM): The BRM provides a framework to facilitate a functional instead of organizational view of the enterprise's lines of business, including the internal operations and services.

- Data Reference Model (DRM): The primary purpose of the DRM is to enable information sharing and reusability across US federal agencies by promoting uniform data management practices and providing a flexible and standards-based approach, which can be applied within a single agency or within a community of interest.

- Application Reference Model (ARM): The ARM provides the basis for categorizing applications and their components to aid agencies in mapping their current and planned information systems, identifying gaps and redundancies, pinpointing opportunities for sharing and reusability, and consolidating information that can be used in conjunction with the other reference models.

- Infrastructure Reference Model (IRM): The IRM provides the taxonomy for categorizing the components of the IT infrastructure, including definitions of technology items within the IT infrastructure and a set of best practices to promote positive outcomes across implementation of the technology.

- Security Reference Model (SRM): Guides the process of weaving in security into all architectural domains across all levels of the enterprise by allowing the architects to classify the security architecture and transform department-specific policies into security controls and measures.

As you can see, each of the four architecture domains are addressed by these models, along with components to address optimal performance, infrastructure, and security. Government entities that could utilize FEAF would include agencies like the Department of Education, HUD, Department of Agriculture, and so on. In fact, the only agencies that would not utilize it are those that can use DoDAF, such as Homeland Security or the Pentagon.

Strengths:

- Very mature framework
- Great reference models that lend to user friendliness

Challenges:

- Cannot be adapted for other levels of government[4]

FEAF is comprehensive and mature enough as a framework that it can be implemented by an agency without needing to fill in gaps like some of the other reference frameworks. In fact, several nations, including India, have also adopted FEAF, proving that it can be successfully implemented by other nations looking to optimize their federal-level agencies.

As a side note, there used to be a separate framework for the Treasury Department known as TEAF, which was instituted starting in 1999 and based upon the Zachman framework. However, as of May 2012, a new federal policy went into effect that laid TEAF to

---

4   There is a separate reference framework used by state government agencies called NASCIO.

rest so that all federal agencies would consistently use FEAF moving forward, with the exception of the Department of Defense.

Conclusion

When implementing an EA strategy, it's key to understand which combination of frameworks will be utilized, especially if you are in one of the industries covered here. An important thing to keep in mind in our increasingly globalized economy is that many of these reference architectures can be utilized on an international level, like ACORD, Frameworx, BIAN, and ARTS.

The common downside for them is that they work best with larger organizations and can prove to be cost prohibitive for a smaller organization. A lack of expertise, skills, and resources can also make these frameworks difficult to implement for smaller organizations. Even so, it is helpful for smaller organizations to know about these frameworks as they lay out their long-term strategy for growth, as there could come a time when utilizing them would make more sense.

As I mentioned before, when we were helping Southeast Regional Bank, we decided to utilize the BIAN reference architecture so that we could integrate some of those industry-specific aspects, not because they could not be addressed by TOGAF® but because BIAN would save time in the process by providing data and direction through industry insights. We could then treat that data and collection of insights as inputs for the appropriate phase of TOGAF® and fill in the gaps BIAN couldn't cover alone. It also helped us identify specific tools and strategies that had already been successful in other banking enterprises, lending confidence to the process.

Now if you are concerned that there is not a reference architecture for your specific industry, there is no need to worry. In the evolution of EA, more reference architectures will certainly come into being over time, but even if one is not available for your industry, you can still benefit from a successful EA transformation through existing frameworks. In the next chapter, we will break down the standard components of Enterprise Architecture to help remove some of the mystery and clarify how it will benefit your enterprise, regardless of industry or size.

CHAPTER TAKEAWAYS

▶ Reference architectures can help you jump-start the EA process. Instead of starting at "zero," you can save a lot of time by using proven methods within your specific industry.

▶ Major reference architectures by industry:

▶ Frameworx = Telecom

▶ BIAN = Banking

▶ ARTS = Retail

▶ DoDAF = Defense

▶ HL7 = Healthcare Providers

▶ ACORD = Insurance

▶ FEAF = Federal Agencies

▶ Many reference architectures can be combined with another architecture framework like TOGAF® or Zachman to address gaps in any domains that are not addressed.

▶ When combining architectures, it's all right to treat industry-specific frameworks as a "buffet" and select the pieces that will help you the most.

▶ Reference architectures are most frequently used by larger organizations since they can be cost prohibitive or experience prohibitive for smaller enterprises.

CHAPTER 4

COMPONENTS OF ENTERPRISE ARCHITECTURE

Have you ever read through the negative reviews on a product online? Perhaps it has a high rating, 4.8 out of a possible 5, but you can't help but look at the handful of low ratings. Usually, you'll find a few people who just want to complain—maybe the product didn't live up to their own imaginary expectations. There will probably be a few people who received a defective product, and then there may be a few who have had genuinely bad experiences that need to be shared as warnings for other potential buyers.

Pick any product you want, any website you want, and you will find someone who had a negative experience, no matter how high the overall rating. This is just human nature—there is no product or service that can make 100 percent of its users perfectly happy. Likewise, there is no one single, proven method for EA that will work 100 percent of the time for 100 percent of companies. The point cannot be overstated: you will have to do some customizing and work to find the perfect fit.

Since many of the reference architectures discussed in the last chapter do not fully address all domains of an enterprise, and because a proven reference architecture does not exist for every industry, it's essential that you have a healthy understanding of the general EA process. This will help you start to see how the process is molded to the enterprise, rather than the enterprise molded to the process. For our purposes, we will rely primarily on the TOGAF® process—first, because it is the industry standard but also because it is so thorough and adaptable across many industries and enterprises.

To go back to our blueprint analogy, we can compare the EA process to the construction process for bringing that blueprint to life. An architect cannot build it on their own but will need tools, supplies, a workforce, and other resources to bring the building off the page and into reality. The architect will meet with a contractor and the business owners—the stakeholders—and will discuss the foundation and framing first since the entire structure will depend upon these.

> An architect cannot build it on their own but will need tools, supplies, a workforce, and other resources.

Once the foundation and framing are decided, they move into deeper details to make sure they have all the tools and resources required to establish a timeline, not only for the completion date but a timeline for each construction phase. Workers will need to be hired, from carpenters to drywall installers, to painters, electricians, plumbers—all the details that will create a fully functioning building.

Throughout the process, there must be clear communication, and the architect and contractor must be able to keep track of all the moving parts to make sure nothing gets overlooked:

- Do we have the proper building permits from the city and state?

- Do we know that heavy equipment is available for laying the foundation?

- Have we accommodated for bad weather scenarios in the timeline?

- Will funding be available at each stage of the project to ensure the work doesn't stall out?

All such questions have to be considered. Likewise, an Enterprise Architect has many components to consider when helping an enterprise through the EA process, especially since each process will be adapted to the enterprise's needs. After all, building a restaurant will have very different architecture requirements from building an accounting office. The same is true for Enterprise Architecture, where the business requirements must be kept in focus.

Now where the EA process differs greatly from this construction analogy is that if the architect discovers a flaw midway through the process, it can be very difficult—and costly—to correct. An advantage of the EA process is that there is opportunity to make adjustments along the way if errors occur or if new needs are identified that were not present in the beginning. This gives the Enterprise Architect the opportunity to adapt the framework to these changes and look ahead in a way that is not always possible for the traditional architect.

A major challenge in the EA process is that we do not usually have the opportunity to help a business build from the ground up. Rather, we are working with an existing enterprise, with existing customers, employees, and resources. We cannot just shut things down to start from scratch, but have to find a way to transform—or "remodel," if you will—the enterprise without shutting it down and without demolishing it.

With Southeast Regional Bank, there was a lot that needed to be transformed. Our job was to look at the current structure, compare it to the new blueprint, and find a way to transform their business into a new structure while still enabling them to serve customers and manage their workforce with minimal interruption. As I mentioned in the last chapter, we were going to accomplish this by utilizing TOGAF® combined with the BIAN reference architecture to help us organize the pieces and put everything back together better than where it started.

So let's look at the components of TOGAF® from a high level so that you can understand how an Enterprise Architect approaches the enterprise and starts to "remodel" it.

The Architectural Development Method (ADM)

A distinguishing feature of the TOGAF® process is the Architecture Development Method (ADM), which is an iterative method or process for developing the specific Enterprise Architectures. Think of this as your approach to sorting and organizing the tools, materials, workforce, and timelines into categories to help you better focus on putting them together in an orderly fashion. There are eight core phases that compose the ADM, along with two supporting phases I will describe later.

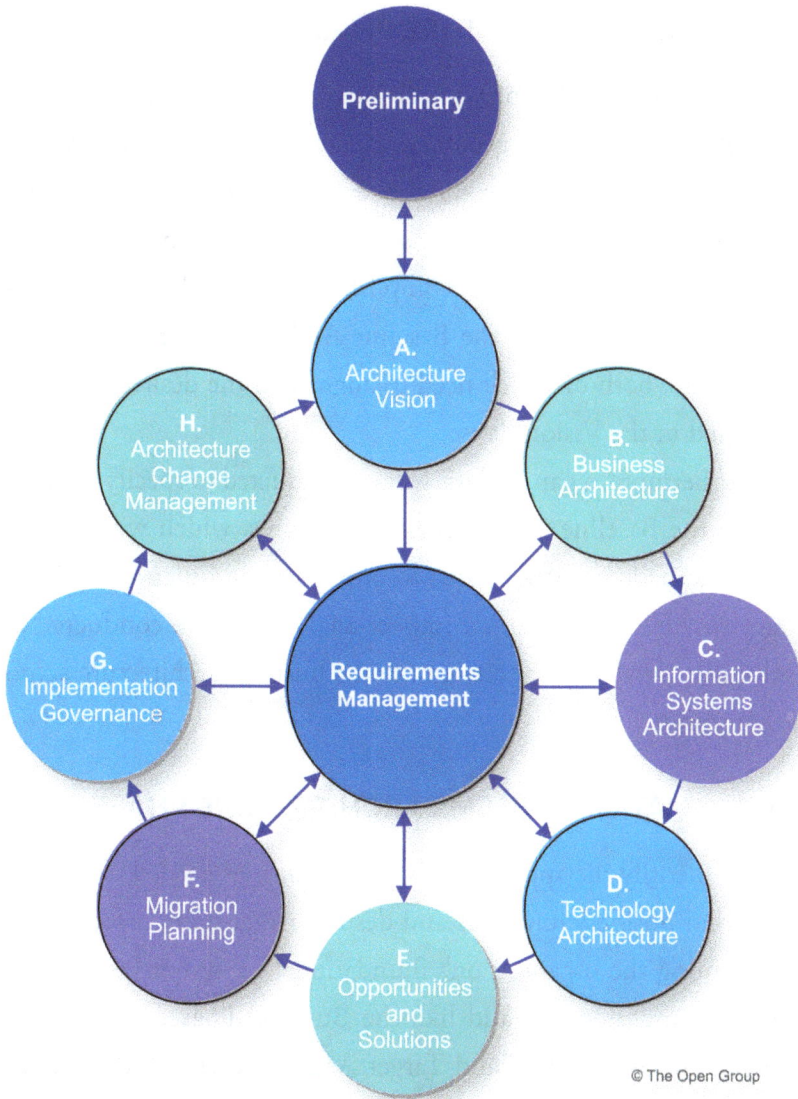

© The Open Group

1. ARCHITECTURE VISION PHASE

This initial phase establishes the scope of the EA, which will include identifying the stakeholders, their requirements, defining the desired outcome (or Architecture Vision), and then obtaining the approval to begin the process itself.

2. BUSINESS ARCHITECTURE PHASE

Just like it sounds, this phase will identify the business functions, capabilities, services, and processes that need to be addressed by the EA, along with the rules for the process and outlining the responsibilities to be carried out. This phase is focused on mapping out how an enterprise will operate to accomplish its goals, including developing descriptions for both the Baseline Architecture and the Target Architecture, both of which need to align with the desired outcome established in the Vision Phase.

Furthermore, a gap analysis will be conducted to specify the gaps between the Baseline and Target Architectures, which will be used to create a roadmap of solutions to implement in order to reach the Target Architecture. Also, an impact analysis will be conducted to resolve the impacts of the changes to the business architecture across the enterprise.

3. INFORMATION SYSTEMS ARCHITECTURE PHASE

Here we identify the applications and data entities needed to support the current business functions and desired target state. It focuses on documenting the organization's foundational IT systems to be used within the architecture, and like the Business Phase, it will build a description of Baseline and Target Architectures, conduct a gap analysis, construct a roadmap, and conduct an impact analysis.

4. TECHNOLOGY ARCHITECTURE PHASE

This phase focuses on identifying the infrastructure and services that will be needed to build the applications and data entities. This includes documenting hardware, software, and other technologies being used to conduct business activities. Again, a description of the Baseline and Target Architectures will be created, a gap analysis conducted, a roadmap built, and an impact analysis conducted.

5. OPPORTUNITIES AND SOLUTIONS PHASE

Now this is the first phase of the ADM process that deals directly with implementing all the deliverables defined and identified in the previous phases by addressing how the business elements will continue to operate during the architectural transitions. It combines all that was done in the previous four phases to develop a high-level roadmap for implementing changes. This will include identifying any transition architectures needed during the transition and defining the Solution Building Blocks (SBBs) for finalizing the Target Architecture.

During this phase, there may be constraints that need to be addressed that could obstruct implementation of new architecture components, and the various gap analyses are consolidated to see if any new gaps are identified and whether any of the previous phases need to be revisited. Furthermore, the Enterprise Architect will assess both the readiness and risk levels for the business transformation. From that, the Enterprise Architect will formulate an implementation and migration strategy to create clear guidelines and communication on how the transformation will take place.

6. MIGRATION PLANNING

In this phase, we finalize the roadmap and identify opportunities and solutions through a cost-benefit analysis and a business value assessment, and through risk management. Specifically, we address how the enterprise will move from the Baseline Architectures to the Target Architectures by finalizing a detailed implementation and migration plan from the one that was started in the previous phase. The Enterprise Architect establishes touch points between various disciplines within the enterprise and prioritizes the identified migration projects aligned with the Architecture Roadmap.

7. IMPLEMENTATION GOVERNANCE

Here the focus shifts to governing the implementation projects and ensuring that they are following the standards and principles established during the previous phases. It defines how the implementation projects may be constrained by the Target Architecture, monitors the implementation while building the architecture, and then creates the signed Architecture Contract. The Enterprise Architect guides the deployment of solutions through a set of deployment resources and conducts compliance reviews to ensure that the implementation conforms to the Target Architecture and catch any potential errors early on.

8. CHANGE MANAGEMENT

The Change Management Phase ensures that any changes to the enterprise's architecture are managed in a controlled manner by categorizing the architecture transformations into three levels:

1. Simplification: Very minor changes, such as code-level changes where none of the architectures are impacted but can be managed by giving a deviation.

2. Incremental: One or more architectures are impacted so that a partial rearchitecting may be required.

3. Rearchitecting: A large change in which all the architectures are impacted and a completely new architecture cycle must be initiated to address them all.

Furthermore, this phase will establish a value realization process, deploy monitoring tools, manage additional risks, provide analysis for the architecture changes, develop change requirements, and activate the process to implement the architecture changes.

In addition to these eight phases, there are two other key components to TOGAF®'s ADM process that play a key role in making sure that the process is not derailed and is set up for success: the Preliminary Phase and the Requirements Management Phase.

> The Change Management Phase ensures that any changes to the enterprise's architecture are managed in a controlled manner.

PRELIMINARY PHASE

This phase is composed of six steps that are carried out before the EA work ever begins. These steps describe the preparation and initiation activities required to create the Architecture Capability, including customizing the architectural framework to the enterprise's needs and defining the initiative's Architecture Principles. We will discuss these aspects of the EA process in more detail in the next chapter.

REQUIREMENTS MANAGEMENT PHASE

Referring to the ADM diagram above, this phase is focused on the process of managing the architecture requirements applying to *all* phases of the ADM, including identifying them, storing them, and then inputting them into each relevant phase. Rather than actually addressing these items, you could think of it as a type of "storage room" for the inputs and outputs of all of the phases to ensure that nothing is being overlooked and that the stakeholder concerns and Architecture Vision are both being kept in focus throughout the entire process.

Content Framework

Each phase of the EA process is composed of content, which, in terms of the enterprise, is the information that already exists and the information needed for the architecture. Going back to the Zachman framework, you can think of the content in terms of the items that would fill in each box of the matrix.

Prior to TOGAF® 9.0, there was no content framework specific to TOGAF®, so Enterprise Architects would commonly utilize Zachman or a similar framework to define the content and TOGAF® to define the process. But now TOGAF® has its own content framework to define what the content should be. You can think of the content framework as a sort of "checklist" of all the things that need to be kept track of or accomplished throughout the entire EA process.

The content framework is made up of two components: the Meta Model and the Work Products.

- The Meta Model lays out the various building blocks that may be included in the architecture and provides a structure for the inputs and outputs created by the ADM. In the diagram on the next page, these are the colored blocks, like "Business Architecture" and "Architecture Realization."

- The Work Products consist of Deliverables, Artifacts, Building Blocks, and other items that have a defined purpose in the architecture and for which templates will be established to create them. In the diagram, these are each of the squares within the colored blocks. For example, within the Business Architecture Meta Model, you see a Work Product labeled "Motivation," which consists of "Drivers," "Goals," "Objectives," and "Measures."

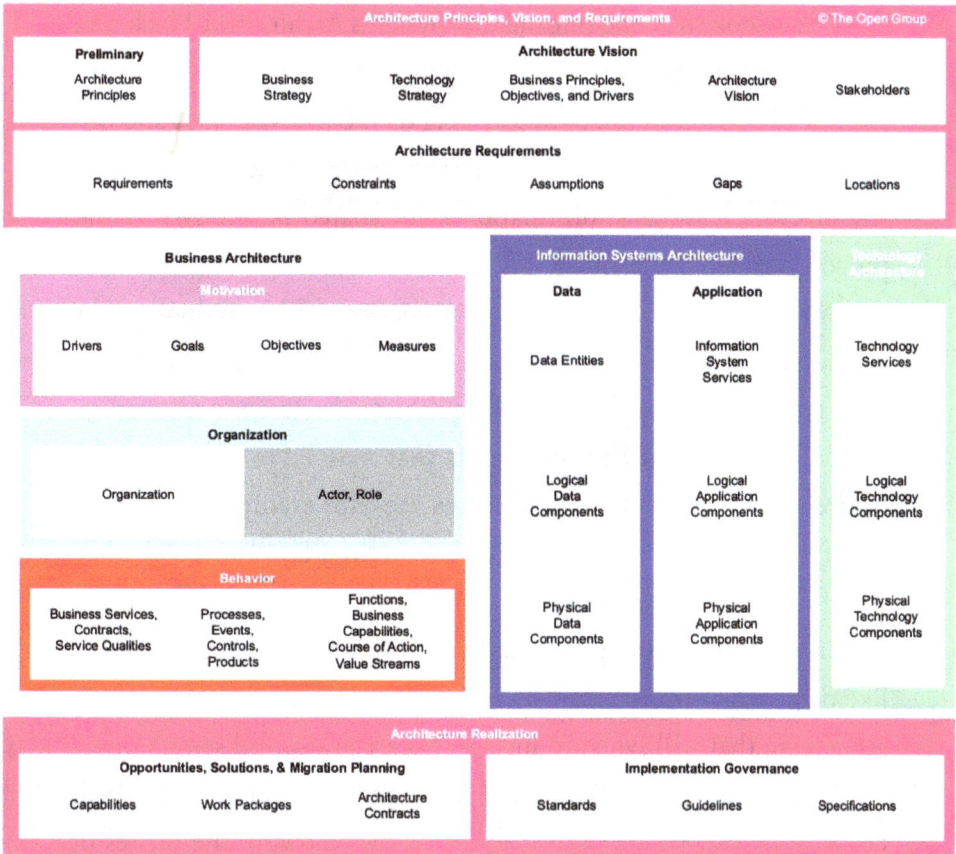

Architecture Principles, Vision, and Requirements					© The Open Group
Preliminary	**Architecture Vision**				
Architecture Principles	Business Strategy	Technology Strategy	Business Principles, Objectives, and Drivers	Architecture Vision	Stakeholders
Architecture Requirements					
Requirements	Constraints		Assumptions	Gaps	Locations

Business Architecture

Motivation			
Drivers	Goals	Objectives	Measures

Organization	
Organization	Actor, Role

Behavior		
Business Services, Contracts, Service Qualities	Processes, Events, Controls, Products	Functions, Business Capabilities, Course of Action, Value Streams

Information Systems Architecture

Data	**Application**
Data Entities	Information System Services
Logical Data Components	Logical Application Components
Physical Data Components	Physical Application Components

Technology Architecture

Technology Services
Logical Technology Components
Physical Technology Components

Architecture Realization

Opportunities, Solutions, & Migration Planning			**Implementation Governance**		
Capabilities	Work Packages	Architecture Contracts	Standards	Guidelines	Specifications

Work Packages

Using these tools, we can start putting together Work Packages to accomplish the EA objectives. A Work Package is a collection of all the building blocks from all four domains of business, data, applications, and technology to address one of the Architecture Principles that needs to be considered in the EA process.

To bring this into context, let's go back to Southeast Regional Bank. One of their Architecture Principles (block at top of diagram) was for there to be shared customer data across the entire enterprise, both for consistency in communication and so that they could cross-sell products to generate new revenue. That is the business domain.

Now, looking at the Information Systems Architecture block, let's discuss the data layer. During the baseline analysis, it would be seen that each business within Southeast Regional Bank was siloed and had their own data management system and process, whereas the Target Architecture is for this information to be shared in one system and process across the enterprise.

So next, we look at the applications layer. We will look at the current applications being utilized—the Baseline Architecture—and what applications may be available to achieve the Target Architecture. We will also look at the constraints that may be in place, such as budgetary restraints or banking regulations, for example.

From there, we then address the technology layer; we will look at specific technology services that will address the requirements identified in the data and applications layers. This could include services like data management, security required by regulations, transaction processing that will sync products with customers, and so on.

This logical grouping of building blocks into Work Packages will be repeated throughout the EA process by following the phases of ADM until all of the EA objectives have been addressed and the Enterprise Architecture has been transformed into the Target Architecture.

Ultimately, the objectives need to be very specific, such as "The enterprise will increase revenue 20 percent by the end of 2022." When we work with an enterprise, we utilize the SMART method to determine whether the objective is strong enough; that is, it must be

- specific,

- measurable,

- actionable,

- realistic, and

- time bound.

REUSABLE BUILDING BLOCKS

Because cross-selling products to increase revenue was also a driver of the EA transformation, the Work Packages developed around the data consolidation need will also come into play in that objective. These are what are known as reusable building blocks because they can be reused and rebuilt within the ADM process and even in future EA transformations.

Organizations often have many components that are not being reused—in my experience, perhaps 10 to 20 percent are actually in use. But by creating an effective Enterprise Continuum, reusability can be significantly increased—I would say by as much as 50 or 60 percent. Reusability is key, as it makes the enterprise more efficient, optimal, and Agile over time.

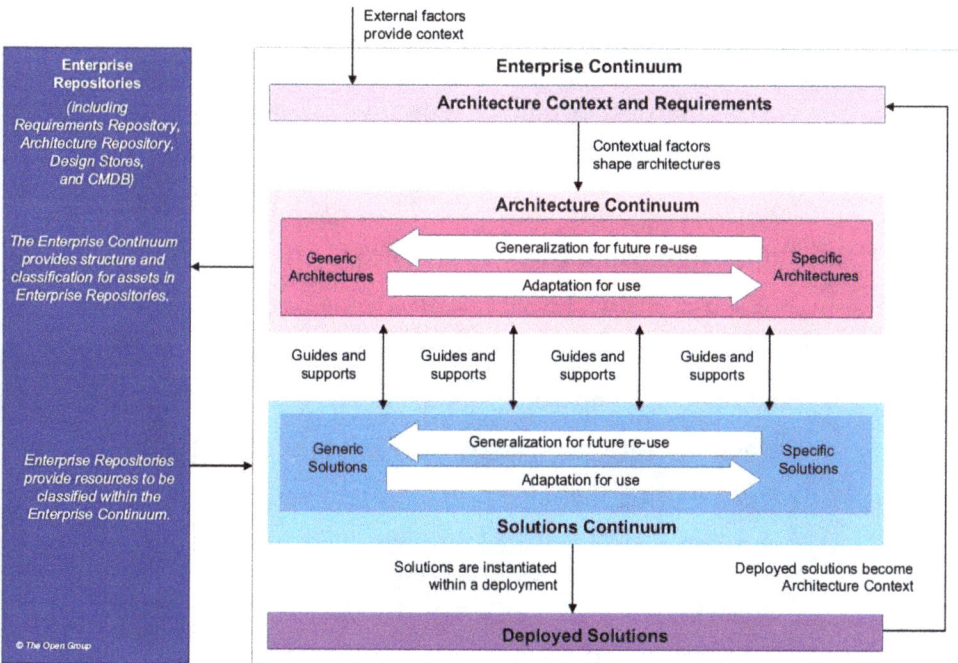

The Enterprise Continuum (EC) serves as a virtual repository containing the architecture assets and solution assets based on their level of reusability. Its role is to provide a model of structure and taxonomy for classifying information and data so that solutions and assets can be identified and then used by the enterprise on a long-term basis.

To be effective, an EC needs to categorize these architecture and solution assets based on their reusability. Typically, four categories are used to rank their reusability as long-term solutions for the enterprise:

- Foundation: These are the most reusable assets and solutions and will include any generic services and functions of the enterprise that more specific architectures and components can be built upon. The Technical Reference Model (TRM) is an example of Foundation Architecture.

- Common Systems: These are the second most reusable assets and solutions and would include any tools utilized to achieve boundaryless information flow between the foundation components. These are usually determined by the Integrated Information Infrastructure Reference Model (III-RM), which is a subset of the TRM. For Southeast Regional Bank, this would look at communications tools that can be standardized across the departments, such as everyone using the same accounting software, everyone utilizing the same CMS, and everyone using the same payroll system and process to limit confusion as data is shared during the EA process.

- Industry-Specific Assets: These are the third most reusable assets and would include any reference architecture being utilized to make the process more industry specific. As I've already mentioned, this would include the decision for us to utilize the BIAN reference architecture in the case of Southeast Regional Bank.

- Organization Specific: These will be the least reusable assets and solutions and will only pertain to the specific enterprise's needs. For Southeast Regional Bank, this would have included updating their payroll procedures for their employees.

Conclusion

While the EA process can be daunting and may be filled with terminology that is new for many, the ADM provides a thorough yet simplified blueprint to assist you in "remodeling" your enterprise. Still, an effective Enterprise Architect will walk with you through the process, ensuring that the business objectives remain centered along the way and that the Target Architecture is achieved with risks managed and objectives achieved in a SMART way.

I know we have yet to discuss how you begin the journey, how you take those first steps to get where you want to be, but I believe it necessary to better understand where you are going first. For the sake of clarity, I've tried to keep to a high-level view of the ADM process so you can dip your toes in the water of the EA process and start to imagine what this would look like to guide your enterprise into long-term growth.

Like any journey in life, it requires a strong sense of vision to know where you want to be. But once you know the destination, the process will provide you with the roadmap and compass to help you every step of the way.

CHAPTER TAKEAWAYS

▶ TOGAF® provides a method or a process known as the Architecture Development Method (ADM), which contains eight phases to address the four architecture domains and the business objectives.

▶ Part of the role of the Enterprise Architect is to increase reusability by identifying what is already available in the industry, either by incorporating a reference architecture into the ADM, or identifying reusable building blocks that will make it a more efficient process.

▶ TOGAF®'s ADM uses a content framework built of Meta Models to help identify content, including assets and solutions.

▶ The Enterprise Continuum (EC) exists as a virtual repository to help keep track of assets and solutions and identify reusable building blocks.

▶ Work Packages are the specific combinations of building blocks identified in the ADM process that are utilized to achieve the objectives.

CHAPTER 5

ARCHITECTURE PRACTICE SETUP

Now that you are more familiar with the major components of TOGAF®'s ADM process as a whole, let's discuss how to start the process and embark on achieving your architecture objectives. To do so, let's go back for a moment to our opening example of physical architecture.

Imagine if an architect were to hand over the blueprint to the contractor but with no discussion about the structure, no discussion about tools, no discussion about materials or the number of personnel. Furthermore, let's imagine that neither of them talk to whoever is paying for the building—no discussion of budget or timeline or resources ... you can imagine how well that would work out.

That is what the architecture practice setup is all about: figuring out what is needed to initiate the process in a way that will pave the way for success and get everyone on the same page. In the case of Southeast Regional Bank, you may recall that their overarching mission was to combine their disparate banking units—retail banking, corporate banking, insurance, investments, loans, etc.—into a one-stop shop. Therefore, the practice that we set up for them needed to reflect the desired architecture functions that should help them to accomplish that mission.

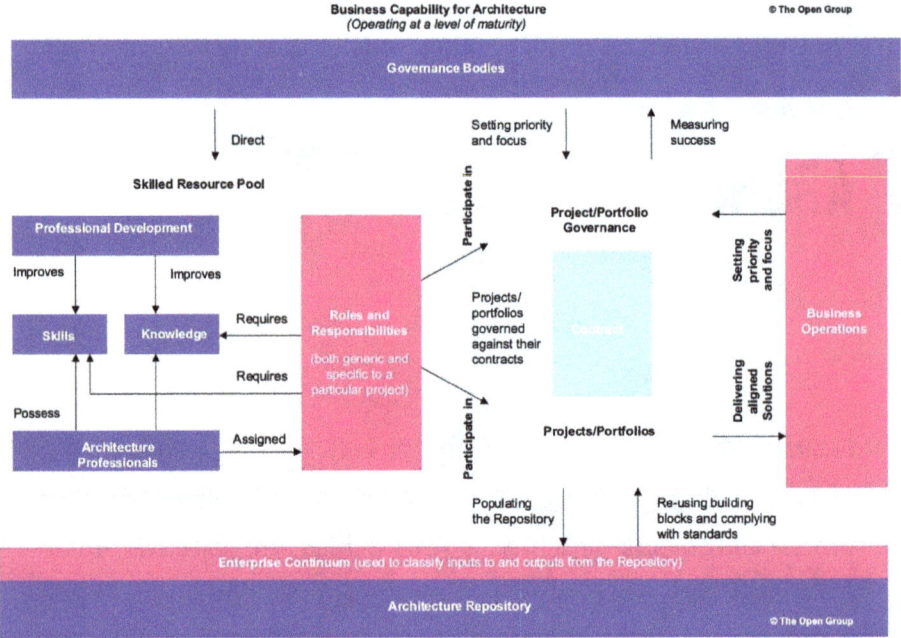

The setup itself is the Architecture Capability Framework (ACF), which is designed to address the needs of a business by applying a consistent plan and guides the automation to set up the architecture practice across all four architecture domains. This enables the Enterprise Architect to ensure that all requirements have been considered as well as identify any potential gaps that the enterprise hasn't noticed on its own.

The Preliminary Phase

In the context of TOGAF®'s ADM, the majority of this work is done in the Preliminary Phase. The ACF does not have to be confined to the Preliminary Phase and may be updated as needed throughout the various phases of the ADM, but you will typically see the initial setup occur during the Preliminary Phase.

We only gave a brief introduction of this phase during the last chapter, not because it is unimportant—quite the contrary. It is so important that it really deserves an entire discussion.

The primary purpose of the Preliminary Phase is to describe the preparation and initiation activities required to create the ACF, including customizing the framework to the enterprise's needs, establishing the architecture's governance, defining the initiative's Architecture Principles, and selecting the EA tools and repository for all of the information being gathered.

This is accomplished through six distinct steps:

1. Scoping the enterprise—that is, identifying which organizations within the enterprise will be impacted and determining exactly who the stakeholders are. Stakeholders can be defined as individuals, teams, or automations that have some interest in or concerns for the system or architecture. Referring to the case of Southeast Regional Bank, the stakeholders could be customers, employees, or even the various systems within each business unit that will be impacted.

2. Confirming the EA governance by creating rules for the process and determining the Support Frameworks for those rules. This step defines the fundamental aspects of managing the enterprise, including the corporate strategy, product strategy, functional strategies, and the IT tactical plans and execution. Additionally, this step will decide who is on the Architecture Board and who will be included on the EA Team, which we will discuss more in the next section.

3. Setting up the EA Team by finding the individuals with the right skills to conduct the EA process. A skills framework will be applied to clearly define the roles and responsibilities for those who are assigned to the EA Team.

Roles	Architecture Board Member	Architecture Sponsor	Enterprise Architecture Manager	Enterprise Architecture Technology	Enterprise Architecture Data	Enterprise Architecture Applications	Enterprise Architecture Business	Program/ Project Manager	IT Designer
Generic Skills									
Leadership	4	4	4	3	3	3	3	4	1
Teamwork	3	3	4	4	4	4	4	4	2
Inter-personal	4	4	4	4	4	4	4	4	2
Oral Communications	3	3	4	4	4	4	4	4	2
Written Communications	3	3	4	4	4	4	4	3	3
Logical Analysis	2	2	4	4	4	4	4	3	3
Stakeholder Management	4	3	4	3	3	3	3	4	2
Risk Management	3	3	4	3	3	3	3	4	1

© The Open Group

4. Defining the Architecture Principles that will provide both standards and consistency across the enterprise throughout the EA process. The Architecture Principles are the rules and guidelines outlining how the enterprise is fulfilling its mission, specifically through the process of architectural changes. These will help guide the decisions that are made to optimize IT assets and create clearer communication and expectations throughout the process.

5. Tailoring the framework for the enterprise's needs, including selection of any industry-specific reference frameworks and incorporating those frameworks into the process. There are several methods for tailoring the framework for the enterprise:

□ Terminology Tailoring, wherein terms are agreed upon and then published as a glossary for the entire organization so that everyone can "speak the same language" and reduce confusion.

▫ Process Tailoring, in which the ADM can be modified in any way by adding, removing, or changing the order of the phases. This can be done by reprioritizing them, customizing them, or adapting them to the changing business environment throughout the process.

▫ Content Tailoring, in which a specific aspect may be focused on over others to direct the process. These aspects could be things like the enterprise's governance, process modeling, data analytics, services, infrastructure consolidation, or even the business motivation.

6. Selecting the tools and techniques necessary to develop the EA Strategy and Implementation Plans, which will also form the repository. This means that the EA Team selects the tools and repository system used for collecting all the data and the established principles being used to tailor the framework to the enterprise's needs. Below you can see some of the most common tools used, along with the evaluation criteria they are designed to meet:

> The EA Team selects the tools and repository system used for collecting all the data.

ENTERPRISE ARCHITECTURE TOOLS					
	Evaluation Criteria				
Tools (Vendor)	Business/ IT Strategy	Gover-nance, Risk, Compliance	Program Management	Enterprise/ IT Portfolio Management	Enterpri Architect & Soluti Architec
HOPEX (Mega)	√	√		√	√
Alfabet, ARIS (Software AG)	√	√	√	√	√
Enterprise Studio (BiZZdesign)	√	√			√
QualiWare EA (QualiWare)	√	√	√	√	√
Abacus (Avolution)	√			√	√
Troux, Planview Enterprise, Projectplace (Planview)	√	√	√	√	√
iServer (Orbus Software)					√
Enterprise Architect (Sparx Systems)					√
ADOIT (BOC Group)					√
System Architect, Focal Point (Unicorn Systems)	√	√	√	√	√

This step enacts a strategy that will reflect the needs and objectives of the enterprise's stakeholders while also empowering the stakeholders to make quick and effective decisions throughout the duration of the architecture change process.

For the sake of our discussion here, though, we will focus on the priorities of the architecture practice setup, which is to establish the Architecture Board, select the EA Team, and set up the repository of tools and architecture assets.

Establishing the Architecture Board

Now we've already defined who the stakeholders are, but it's important to understand that this is a different group than the Architecture Board. For example, when conducting the architecture changes for Southeast Regional Bank, some of the stakeholders included the sales staff who would have new opportunities to bundle products and upsell products to boost revenue, but they did not play a governance role on the Architecture Board.

Among the stakeholders is the Sponsor Stakeholder, the individual who granted approval to begin the process and has a vested interest in its success. For example, this could be the CFO who has signed off on the budget for the architecture process to begin, especially if the goal of the process is to help the enterprise increase revenue. In other situations, it could be the CIO who has an interest in seeing the IT infrastructure of the enterprise streamlined.

The Architecture Board, on the other hand, can be thought of similar to a board of directors or a steering committee that governs the architecture. The board makes decisions about what is right for the enterprise, what is wrong for the enterprise, and whether the established standards are being followed throughout the process. Members of the Architecture Board may belong to a group of stakeholders that will be impacted, of course, but they are a very different level of stakeholder since they are overseeing, or sponsoring, the process.

Again, you might think of it like a Board of Trustees for a nonprofit. Typically, each member of the Board of Trustees has work they do outside of the nonprofit—they may be business owners, public officials, or community leaders—but they are not actually performing the work being done by the nonprofit. Certainly, they have an interest in the success of the nonprofit and provide accountability and guidance for the direction of the nonprofit's staff, even though they are not directly supervising the work.

This is the same type of function that an Architecture Board will perform for the enterprise. They are individuals that still have other responsibilities within the enterprise and therefore may not be involved in the day-to-day process of the architectural changes taking place, but they will be the ones to make sure that resources are available and that the rules are being followed by the EA Team.

Responsibilities of the Architecture Board:

- They provide a basis for all of the decision making as it pertains to architecture transformations.

- They ensure there is consistency between all of the sub-architectures.

- They determine targets for the reusability of components within the architecture.

- They guarantee that the Enterprise Architecture is flexible enough to address changing business needs and also leverage new technologies.

- They enforce compliance of the architecture.

- They improve the architecture maturity level throughout the enterprise.

- They ensure the adoption of discipline in regard to architecture-based development.

- They support the escalation capability for any out-of-bounds decisions in a visible way.

So let's take a moment to look at these responsibilities from a practical view. Let's say for a moment that one of the implementation teams assigned to a specific project wants to deviate from the standards of what is dictated by the EA Compliance Criteria. Before they can do anything else, they have to bring an exception request to the board for approval.

The board will take the request under consideration and decide whether the deviation can be allowed or not. Will it violate an external standard, such as a state or federal law? Is it aligned with the vision of the project's internal standards? Is the deviation architecture based in that it will improve a target domain? Does it help lead the organization to a more mature architecture? All of this will be considered before the board will give approval.

As you can imagine, this could sometimes frustrate the implementation team. Perhaps they wanted to use a new technology that had just become available but were denied permission to do so. Maybe this was because it was not in the budget, or perhaps there is uncertainty about whether the new technology will integrate with other technology that has already been approved. Or perhaps the team does *not* want to use the new technology and is resistant to its implementation. After all, it's not unusual for there to be reluctance to change within the architecture, but as the business or the technology transforms, then the architecture must transform as well.

The board may or may not explain their rationale to the implementation team, but the team will have to go along with the board's decision because going rogue and making their own decisions without approval could derail the entire process and lead to failure. Ensuring compliance can prove one of the most challenging responsibilities. As a best practice, I find it's best for the board to make it a primary concern to educate and encourage the implementation teams to self-regulate and be compliant on their own. Clear communication on the purpose of the changes goes a long way in reducing friction between the board and implementation teams.

> As the business or the technology transforms, then the architecture must transform as well.

Another practical example of the role of the board in relation to the EA Team is ensuring consistency between the sub-architectures of the enterprise. With Southeast Regional Bank, the sub-architectures would be business components such as the MDM (Master Data Management), the CRM (Customer Relations Management), and Finance. In the process of mapping out the new enterprise structure, there will be overlaps between these components, so there must be consistency to make sure that changes will integrate smoothly with the CRM.

For example, if a new automated bill payment system is being integrated into the CRM so that customers can customize their own payment options, the finance department needs to be involved to ensure that the transactions will not get lost in cyberspace but will transfer seamlessly through whatever transaction application is being implemented.

Furthermore, the Architecture Board will help set a target for establishing reusable components throughout the enterprise for optimal performance. As I mentioned before, most organizations that I have worked with have 10 to 20 percent reusable components in their baseline Enterprise Architecture, where they need to have a goal of at least 50 to 60 percent.

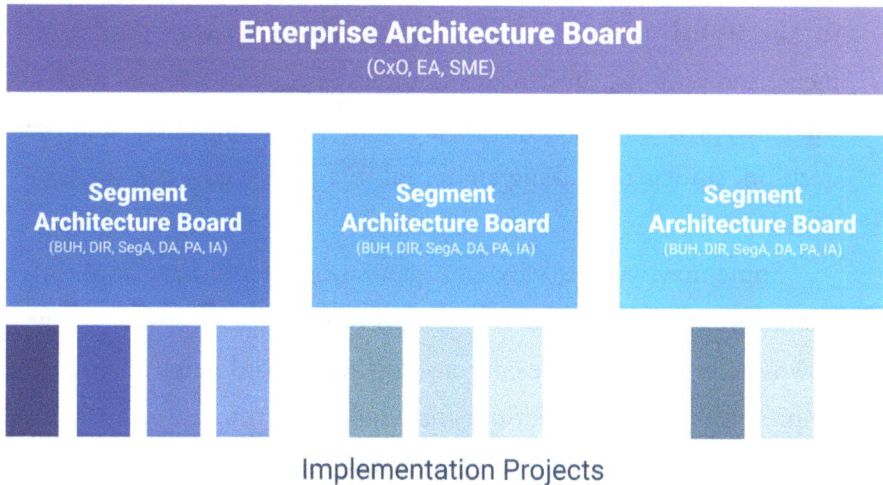

Enterprise Architecture Board
(CxO, EA, SME)

Segment Architecture Board
(BUH, DIR, SegA, DA, PA, IA)

Segment Architecture Board
(BUH, DIR, SegA, DA, PA, IA)

Segment Architecture Board
(BUH, DIR, SegA, DA, PA, IA)

Implementation Projects

And finally, the board should support a visible escalation capability for out-of-bounds decisions, meaning that there can be levels of governance established to better monitor the decision-making process.

As seen in the graphic above, there can be one Architecture Board approving the entire process at the Enterprise Level, but they could choose to establish additional boards at Segment Levels within the enterprise and then at Program Levels. In the case of Southeast Regional Bank, they could have set up a board for each business segment, like HR, Finance, Data Management, and so on (Segment Level in graphic). In other words, the Segment Architecture Boards don't necessarily correlate to business units or departments but to specific program functions or business capabilities that are being impacted by the architecture change. The Segment Boards could then oversee the specific implementation projects that have a direct impact upon their segment with more involvement than what the Enterprise-Level Architecture Board is capable of doing.

Rather than complicate the process, this can actually create a structure of checks and balances. For example, if the Segment Architecture Boards make a decision that is not in favor of the implementation projects, those teams can then escalate to a higher level—the Enterprise-Level Architecture Board—and appeal for another decision, similar to making an appeal to a higher court in the legal world.

Some may wonder why an organization should have an Architecture Board at all. Some may feel as though setting one up slows down the process. On the contrary, having a board helps offset costs by preventing one-off solutions that could slow things down when a more reusable solution could be identified. Taking the time to set up a board in the beginning saves time in the long run.

There is also great value in having a board since they can prevent unconstrained developments which might otherwise lead to problems such as the following:

- High costs of development, operation, and support due to numerous run-time environments, languages, interfaces, or protocols

- Lower-quality architecture due to a lack of checks and balances

- Higher risk of failure from a lack of consistent principles to follow

- Difficulty in replicating and reusing solutions

From a TOGAF® perspective, the stakeholders are identified during the Vision Phase rather than in the Preliminary Phase; however, the Preliminary Phase will identify the high-level stakeholders, such as the Architecture Board members and the Sponsor Stakeholder. Once the board is established, then it will become their job to set up the EA Team.

Selection of the Enterprise Architecture Team

In short, the EA Team is the collection of individuals who will actually be conducting and executing the work of the architecture changes. The two most important aspects of setting up the EA Teams are to ensure that they have the necessary skills to tailor the framework for the desired outcome and that they represent a diversity of perspectives and disciplines within the enterprise.

To go back to Southeast Regional Bank, since their HR systems were going to be impacted by the other changes being made to streamline communication within the enterprise, it was essential to include a member of the human resources team so that those details would not be overlooked. Likewise, they needed to ensure that the EA Team included someone from compliance who could verify that banking regulations were being followed throughout the process. If nothing else, this is essential for mitigating risks, but there is great value in having diverse perspectives to prevent details of the business from being overlooked.

It's important to note that there may be some overlap between the Architecture Board and the EA Team, especially depending on the size of the organization. For example, the Director of IT for the enterprise may be on the board but could also be a member of the EA Team since optimization of the IT solutions is already a part of their day-to-day responsibilities.

In TOGAF®, a specific skills framework is utilized to identify the skills that are needed on the EA Team. Rather than basing the selection of the EA Team on individuals, it is instead focused on the skills themselves. This is essential because it can be all too easy for an enterprise to line up an EA Team based on whom the board knows or based solely on job titles. But the best results will come from assembling the right talent for the right architecture.

> There is great value in having diverse perspectives to prevent details of the business from being overlooked.

From there, it is the EA Team that will actually be selecting the initiatives and projects that need to be done to build the new architecture, understanding that these initiatives must be approved by the Architecture Board first. Once more, this sets up a system of checks and balances throughout the process.

In addition to the initiatives, the EA Team is also responsible for selecting and setting up the third component of the architecture practice setup, which is the repository.

Setting Up the Repository

The repository is a physical model whose job is to store the architecture and solution assets, which is accomplished through an EA tool. Having such a tool will not only improve communication and reduce confusion but will also help the EA Team in identifying reusable solutions that can make the process faster and more cost effective.

The Architecture Repository supports the Enterprise Continuum (EC), which we discussed in the last chapter, by providing it with physical storage of architecture assets. This will include everything pertaining to the EA process from the various architectures being impacted, the business processes, the IT and business solutions, regula-tory requirements, organizational standards, service level agreements, and so on. This information will feed into and inform every stage of the process—from development, to implementation, to deploy-ment—to create consistency throughout the architectural changes.

Enterprise Repository

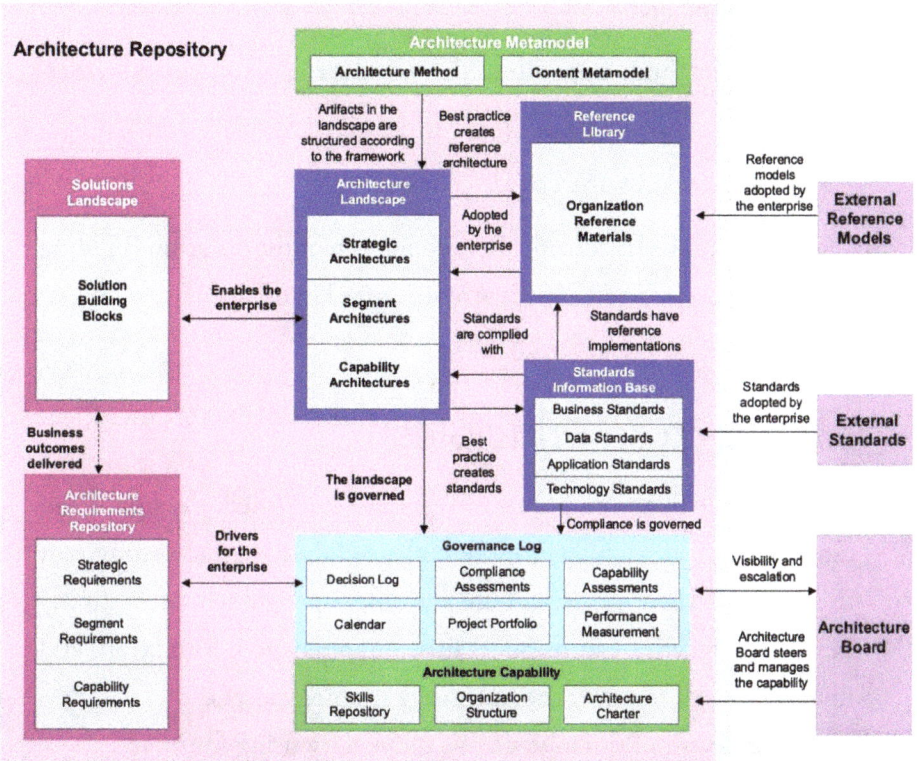

As detailed above, the repository is made up of multiple components:

- Architecture Metamodel: ADM, Content Metamodel
- Architecture Capability: Parameters, Skills, Organization Structure for Governance of the Repository

- Architecture Landscape: The enterprise's building blocks, including Strategic-, Segment-, and Capability-Level building blocks

- Reference Library: Guidelines and templates to create the new architecture

- Standards Information Base (SIB): List of specifications for compliance

- Governance Log: Stores the outputs of governance activities

- Architecture Requirements Repository: All requirements approved by the board

- Solutions Landscape: Representation of the Solution Building Blocks supporting the Architecture Landscape

Architecture Principles

Once the EA Board and the EA Team are confirmed, the board will establish a set of Architecture Principles to be adhered to throughout the process. These principles are the rules and guidelines outlining how the enterprise will fulfill its mission, organize information, and make decisions to select the optimal technology assets.

Architecture Principles can be defined by using four parts:

- **Name**: Represents the essence of the rule and should be something memorable.

- **Statement**: The "What" of the principle, which should succinctly and clearly communicate the fundamental rule.

- **Rationale**: The "Why" of the principle, highlighting the business benefits of adhering to the principle using business terminology and relationships to any other principles. The rationale also prioritizes the principles based on relevance to the enterprise's mission.

- **Implications**: The "How," which should highlight the requirements for both the business and IT for carrying out the principles and consequences, emphasizing the ultimate impact to the stakeholders.

When putting together the principles, there are five criteria or qualities that distinguish a good set of principles:

- **Understandable**: They are clear and unambiguous.

- **Robust**: They enable the enterprise as a whole to make better decisions.

- **Complete**: They address all aspects of the business and its IT needs.

- **Consistent**: They should not be contradictory across business units so as to minimize confusion.

- **Stable**: They should be developed with an intent to be long lasting and with consideration for their reusability.

With Southeast Regional Bank, one of the guiding Architecture Principles for their process was the need for Business Continuity. After all, they could not discontinue their everyday services or forgo revenue generation for the duration of the EA process, so there had to be a plan in place for how business could continue to operate as seamlessly as possible while the various changes were being implemented. Therefore, the EA Board would have defined a principle for the EA Team to follow such as the following:

PRINCIPLE	Business Continuity
STATEMENT	The operations of all business units within Southeast Regional Bank will be maintained even in the event of any disruptions to the system.
RATIONALE	The key stakeholders in applying technology to meet business needs are any information users within Southeast Regional Bank, such as employees, but can also include customers accessing their private information. To ensure that information management is synced within the enterprise, it is essential that every organization in the enterprise be involved in every element of the information environment. Business experts from each segment of the enterprise need to team up with the technical staff tasked with the development and maintenance of the information environment with the objective of defining the goals of IT.
IMPLICATIONS	To function as a team, each stakeholder must take responsibility for the development of the information environment. Implementation of this principle will require resources.

While these principles are established in the Preliminary Phase of the EA process, they will be referred to and revisited throughout to ensure consistency in decision making as well as setting up a system of checks and balances. When aligned with the appropriate EA tool selected by the EA Team, the principles will help ensure that implementation goes more smoothly and will align with the needs of the enterprise.

Conclusion

Organizational Structure

Governance Environment

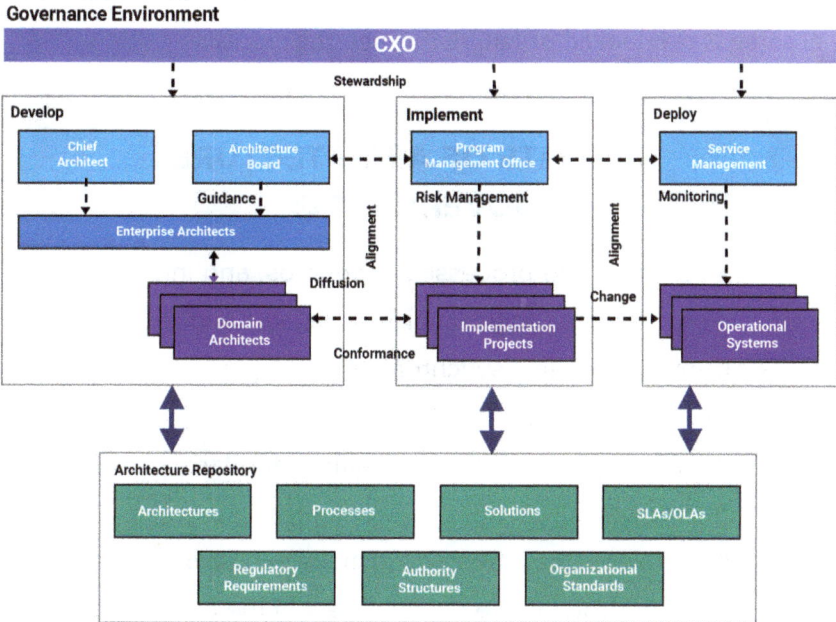

Above is an example of what the governance structure could look like. At the top, you find the Sponsor Stakeholder granting approval for the process, typically a member of the C-Suite, such as the CIO or CTO. Below, in the Develop section, you find the Chief Architect, who would probably be a chairperson to the board to guide the Enterprise Architects—who, in turn, are guiding domain architects.

These domain architects are guiding the implementation projects to be compliant with the Enterprise Architecture. Meanwhile, in the Implement section, the Program Management Office conducts governance from a risk management perspective. On the right, in the

Deploy section, you have Service Management, which provides governance after the projects have been implemented. This is where Operations and Service Management will monitor the operating systems. At the bottom, you'll find the repository to store all of the various information that has been collected for each phase and ensure that nothing is overlooked or falling through the cracks.

BENEFITS OF ARCHITECTURE GOVERNANCE:

- It connects the processes, resources, and information directly to the organization's objectives and strategies.
- It integrates and synchronizes best practices across the organization.
- It promotes alignment with standard industry frameworks.
- It empowers the enterprise to make full use of its assets.
- It better protects the digital assets of the enterprise.
- It supports both best practice and regulatory requirements.
- It encourages risk management in a tangible way.

Too often, I have seen organizations skip this step and think they can transform their architecture without a formal setup. Unfortunately, this typically leads to either failure of the process or, at best, wasted time and money as they realize that they need to start all the way over.

With a complicated situation like Southeast Regional Bank, the architecture practice setup was key to their success in maintaining good communication, making informed decisions, and transforming their business. But no matter the size or industry of your organization, setting up a solid architecture practice is the foundation for any EA initiative.

In general, the setup of the architecture practice should be a fairly short process. In my experience, most enterprises are able to get the practice setup done within a few weeks up to a few months at the longest. With a strong board, a skilled EA Team, and a supportive repository, you increase the chances of a successful architecture initiative. Conversely, if you try to skip this initial step or don't have enough skills represented, or you don't have the right team, then it will be very difficult to succeed.

CHAPTER TAKEAWAYS

▶ The first step of the architecture practice setup is establishing an Architecture Board, a group that will initiate and grant approval for decisions throughout the EA process.

▶ The EA Team is set up by the Architecture Board based on the skills needed for the architecture transformation.

▶ There may be some overlap between the EA Board and the EA Team, depending on the size of the organization and scope of the architecture change. The most senior members of the EA Team will be included on the board in most situations.

▶ The EA Team should be made up of a mix of perspectives and include members from each discipline within the enterprise to ensure that all aspects of the architecture are covered.

▶ The EA Team needs to select the right EA tool (a repository) to store the assets, solutions, and other artifacts collected throughout the phases of the EA process.

▶ Architecture Principles are established by the EA Board for the EA Team to help guide the process, establishing consistency and clear communication throughout all phases of implementation.

CHAPTER 6

SELECTING THE RIGHT APPROACH

In traditional architecture, the architect takes a largely passive role once the blueprint is passed off to the contractor for the building process to begin. They may be consulted throughout the construction process as issues arise, but they are no longer playing a day-to-day role.

When architecting an enterprise, however, the Enterprise Architect remains very involved from beginning to end, not only designing the "blueprint" through the selection of the right framework for the enterprise's transformation but also playing a role in making decisions and implementing new tools and processes. Therefore, it is at this juncture in our discussion where we must deviate even further away from how Enterprise Architecture compares to traditional architecture.

As mentioned in the last chapter, one of the Architecture Principles for Southeast Regional Bank was "Business Continuity." As you can imagine, this is a guiding principle for most businesses going through an architectural transformation. But to attain Business Continuity while optimizing systems, especially in a case as complex as Southeast Regional Bank, it was important to decide *how* to approach the transformation. Having the right framework selected, the right board and team, is essential, of course, but so is the approach.

As the saying goes, there is "more than one way to skin a cat," so knowing how you will approach implementation is a key ingredient in starting the transformation process. The ideal approach should ensure that transformation occurs as easily as possible but without business disruption. Therefore, one of the key aspects in which we Enterprise Architects are often put to great use in the EA process is selecting the right approach for how the enterprise will implement changes.

Having the right framework selected, the right board and team, is essential, of course, but so is the approach.

In my professional experience, there are two types of approaches to EA: Baseline First and Target First.

Baseline First

As you may have already assumed, a Baseline First approach is one that begins with the baseline of the architecture—that is, what the enterprise already has in place "as is." It may also be referred to as an Incremental Improvements Approach and, in my own experience, tends to be the most common type of approach used.

Here the EA Board and Team will analyze the current state of things, including what works and what doesn't, and then create a list of improvement areas. From there, they will look at implementing improvements in the areas that were identified to reach the desired state.

This approach is ideal when an enterprise wants to make some incremental improvements, especially when they come to the point of realizing that there are some problem areas. Perhaps there have been a lot of complaints or incidents with a particular process, revealing that the process is broken, and the enterprise needs to fix that one component rather than overhaul the entire organization.

In order to fix the problem, this approach employs a straightforward method:

- Understand the process.

- Identify the pain points/problems.

- Address the pain points/problems.

The Baseline First approach is often useful in identifying a reference architecture that may fix the problem. In the case of Southeast Regional Bank, a baseline approach toward a broken process would have pointed them to the BIAN framework in order to identify some benchmarks in the industry that could be applied without having to come up with all of the solutions from scratch. The same could be said for a company in telecom utilizing Frameworx to address a recurring customer service issue or a retail enterprise referencing ARTS to fix an inventory process problem.

Within a baseline approach, there are a couple of prominent optimization techniques that can be considered.

SIX SIGMA

Developed by engineer Bill Smith in 1986, Six Sigma is a specific set of techniques and tools for improving processes, focused on eliminating errors and defects in a process in order to increase and maximize the efficiency of the process.

Individuals can be certified in the Six Sigma process and can be hired by a company to help them improve a process, or some companies will even have a Six Sigma specialist as part of their staff. In the context of an EA process, it is helpful to have a process expert involved in some capacity. Whether they are on the EA Board or not will depend upon the enterprise and breadth of the architecture work being accomplished.

In some cases, an enterprise may identify the specific areas requiring a Six Sigma approach and bring in a Six Sigma specialist to lead in those areas, even if they are not involved in other areas of EA optimization. This is because Six Sigma has certain distinctions that do not exist in other process-optimization techniques, including the following:

- A belief that business success can be achieved by standardizing processes to make them stable and predictable through reducing process variation

- A belief that business processes should be defined, measured, analyzed, improved, and controlled

- A belief that long-term improvement requires enterprise-wide commitment, especially from the top level of management

- A focus on achieving measurable financial returns

- A focus on management and leadership support

- A focus on making decisions based on statistical methods and verifiable data, not assumptions

So let's say a business wants to improve its manufacturing process. A Six Sigma approach will look at things such as how many defects occur in the assembly of the product, how often, and whether those defects can be attributed to a specific step in the process. Then they will look to eliminate those errors by making changes such as upgrading technology, using improved materials, or improvement in staff training. By decreasing defects and errors, one should see an increase in profitability, as fewer materials are wasted on defective products and through more efficient use of time.

While there are several different methodologies that can be employed to help an enterprise approach processes through Six Sigma, they all hold these core beliefs and foci, using data to identify errors, eradicate them, and establish a more efficient and financially beneficial process.

LEAN

Originally developed by Toyota to eliminate inefficiency in the company's manufacturing process, the Lean technique is focused on finding waste in a process and removing it. Here there is an examination of the steps in the process to see which ones fail to add value to the customer or end user and then eliminate those activities. In this way, it is efficiency focused like Six Sigma, but it also has qualities that concentrate on building a respectful work culture in which employees are enabled to pursue improvement and share any ideas they develop for continuous improvement.

05. PURSUIT PERFECTION

04. ESTABLISH PULL

LEAN PRINCIPLES

01. DEFINE VALUE

03. CREATE FLOW

02. MAP VALUE STREAM

There are five key principles for the Lean technique:

- Identify Value: This is defined specifically from the customer view—that is, what the customer's needs are for a specific product or service.

- Map the Value Stream: Once the value is determined, then there is a mapping of all the steps and processes involved, from collecting and assembling the raw materials for a product, to taking it to market for the customer. The goal here is to identify any steps in the process that do not add value and find ways to remove or consolidate those steps. This may sometimes be referred to as "reengineering" and should result in a better understanding of the business operation as a whole.

> The Lean technique is focused on finding waste in a process and removing it.

- Create Flow: After the wasteful steps have been removed, this principle looks at the remaining steps and ensures they flow smoothly from one to the other without interruptions to the overall process. The goal is to see a verifiable increase in the productivity and efficiency of the process, leading to more profitability.

- Establish Pull: This principle refers to the idea of the customer being able to "pull" the product from the business as needed because it is more available or more easily accessible. This pull should be achieved with an improved process flow that allows for customer demand to be met, thereby establishing additional value.

- Seek Perfection: One might see this as the most important step because it is the core concept of making Lean thinking for process improvement a part of the corporate culture. In seeking perfection, the idea is that every employee is involved in perfecting the business and can contribute to process improvement over the long term.

There are many Lean techniques, one of the most popular being Kaizen, which is focused upon incremental improvement by taking a process, identifying what smaller actions can be taken to improve the process, and continuously repeating this until you achieve an optimized process. There does not need to be a major initiative occurring for it to take place; rather, it is intended to become a part of the ongoing mindset and culture of the company, always looking for how to improve things for the benefit of the customer.

To use our previous example of manufacturing, a Lean technique would assess the manufacturing process by looking at how quickly products make it to market for customers and whether they are satisfied with those products. Therefore, the enterprise will look at each step of the process to see where waste may exist, from wasted materials to wasted time in delivery, and so on. They will also look for the connections between customer satisfaction and how that can be increased through process changes. By making incremental improvements in each area of waste, customer demand can be better satisfied and lead to more profit.

Taking this customer-first view of the process helps the enterprise take a look outside itself and identify those areas that employees may have become complacent to or steps that are outdated and no longer serve a function in serving the customer. This should create a more enjoyable customer experience, resulting in higher satisfaction and repeat business. This aspect of repeat business is especially important, as it is more profitable for a business to keep a customer than it is to seek out new ones. Lean may also be a more desirable technique for those enterprises that want all of their employees involved in the long-term improvement of the business—not only the top-level leadership.

Often, enterprises will combine both Six Sigma and Lean techniques when optimizing a process rather than select one over the other. No organization is without problems in their processes, so there is always room for improvement. More often than not, they just have "blind spots," which these techniques can help reveal. In fact, I personally have found this combination of techniques to be beneficial and reusable for enterprises.

For example, let's say a manufacturer has manufactured a million parts, but 50 percent of those are coming back as defective. Obviously, the enterprise will want to improve upon this to eliminate defects and waste in the process. In a situation like this, there could be multiple factors contributing to the problem, so a combination of the two techniques will help them analyze the baseline and see what can be improved upon. Perhaps there is machinery that needs to be updated, or perhaps there are supply chain delays that need to be addressed.

From an IT perspective, a company might be looking at the systems they have in place that accomplish the same purpose and look for opportunities to streamline or consolidate. Maybe they have multiple HR systems across business units; maybe different departments are using different CMS applications, leading to a breakdown in communication and wasted time and resources.

As you might imagine, this is the type of approach that was taken with consolidating system operations for Southeast Regional Bank. In general, an enterprise going through a Baseline First approach, whether they are utilizing Six Sigma or Lean techniques, can think of the process in three simple steps:

- Collect the necessary information.

- Analyze the information.

- Find what can be consolidated/eliminated.

BASELINE FIRST AND THE FOUR DOMAINS

Before we move on from the Baseline First approach, I think it's important to consider how this approach interacts with the four architecture domains. As a reminder, these four domains are business, data, applications, and technology. In a full EA process, all four of these domains should be considered in the process of optimization.

Similar to the Lean approach detailed previously, if the enterprise is using a Baseline First approach, then they don't know what the Target Architecture looks like in terms of the four domains. This means that they must go "bottom up," beginning with what they *do* know: the existing architectures for business, data, applications, and technology.

They will gather that information and analyze it and then, from that analysis, make a decision of what they want their Target Architecture to look like. This will then allow them to focus on the specific incremental changes that need to be made in each of the four domains.

Target First

A Target First, or radical change, approach is one that looks at changing things not at an Incremental or Process Level but at an Enterprise Level. Typically, this would be done when a major change needs to happen across multiple layers or business units of the enterprise or when a change in the industry or market has taken place.

In my opinion, "business as usual" is always a dangerous mentality. History has shown that businesses that fail to innovate or adapt to changes in their industry tend to fall by the wayside, and the same can be said of those who ignore "little problems," which eventually snowball into financially devastating problems.

A Target First approach seeks to avoid this by looking for radical improvements that can be made to remain innovative. There is nothing wrong with making small changes here and there to improve on a Process Level, but sooner or later, a competitor may develop a radical innovation that changes the industry. *When* that happens—not if—then there is always the chance that they take over the industry and take away the market share you used to count on.

A great example of this can be seen in the world of car manufacturing. Until recently, the major American car manufacturers felt comfortable with their share of the market and felt confident in their year-to-year performance. In a sense, they felt too big to fail, and I think most of the business world would have agreed with them.

But then Tesla entered the market with their innovative designs for the electric vehicle. While they certainly did not create the idea of the electric car, they found a way to create products that could appeal to a larger population than just eco-minded consumers. In fact, Tesla's annual sales increased from "$400 million in 2012 to $31.5 billion in 2020."[5] Numbers like that have forced major legacy auto manufacturers to look at how investing more in EVs would help their bottom line heading into the future.

Other radical Target First approaches may be brought about by needing to overhaul the business or streamline the business as the

---

5   "Who Are Tesla's Biggest Competitors?," Manufacturing.net, accessed April 20, 2021.

result of acquisitions or mergers. This was exactly the situation with Southeast Regional Bank, in their acquisition of multiple business units and then looking to transform into a one-stop shop for banking and financial services. This was not a transformation that could be achieved simply on an Incremental or Process Level.

Now that is not to say that, in the scope of a full EA process, an enterprise will not use both. In the case of Southeast Regional Bank, a radical Target First approach was necessary to create a single view of the customer and streamline the organization as a whole. But to understand everything that they had as an enterprise and figure out how to bring all of the pieces together, it was necessary to use a Baseline First approach on the individual processes.

Whether the radical change is brought about by an external driver—like Tesla's impact on the auto market—or an internal driver such as Southeast Regional Bank, the heart of Target First is innovation. In my experience, there are two predominant types of innovations that drive the change: technology innovation and business model innovation.

TECHNOLOGY INNOVATION

An innovation in technology is one of the purest forms of a Target First approach. This can occur at any time new technology is emerging in the market that will make an impact upon an industry. This could include things like AI being used in industries like engineering or blockchain within the realm of cryptocurrency.

Essentially, the approach is driven by a desire of the enterprise to remain competitive within their industry by harnessing emerging technology. Time and time again, history has proved that the enterprises that implement innovative technology will survive and grow, while companies hesitant to innovate are often left behind. A perfect example can be found in the downfall of Blockbuster Video when they failed to invest in online entertainment developments that paved the way for the current "streaming wars."

Or you might think of a bank looking to update their mobile app options for customers, both for improving their customer service experience and maximizing revenue generation. They will look at where they want to be—a customer-friendly banking app—and utilize emerging technology solutions to achieve their target.

BUSINESS MODEL INNOVATION

Meanwhile, an innovation in the business model of the enterprise could be classified as a radical change approach. This will occur when something happens in the marketplace that prompts transformation in the business model itself. This includes the shift of consumer spending from brick-and-mortar physical locations to online marketplaces. For example, there are now entire retail businesses that exist wholly online, such as Stitch Fix and ThreadUp, something that would have been unthinkable in the retail industry twenty years ago.

Or the innovation could be driven by the appearance of new competition, such as the hotel industry revisiting their business model because of the appearance of new competitors like Airbnb or the taxi industry seeing the emergence of services like Uber and Lyft.

Any kind of shakeup in an industry has the potential to lead to business model innovation, during which the enterprise must look at how they will face the change and remain competitive. While there may be a technology component to the innovation that is happening, the main impetus for the innovation is rooted in the business model itself and adapting to changing customer needs.

Once again, Baseline First has been the more common approach utilized in my own experience, especially when an enterprise is looking at their own operations and how they can become more efficient and adaptable. Target First and radical change approaches are rarer since they are typically necessary only when there is a major change in technology or business model. But when a Target First approach is being taken, it will generally also involve some Baseline First approaches being taken for specific initiatives on a Project or Implementation Level.

TARGET FIRST AND THE FOUR DOMAINS

As we did with Baseline First, we need to take a look at how a Target First approach interacts with the four architecture domains before we can conclude this topic. As described previously, since the Target First approach is a radical one, impacting all areas of the enterprise, the target is already defined by the vision of where the enterprise wants to be.

> Any kind of shakeup in an industry has the potential to lead to business model innovation.

Starting from the vision, the enterprise then works downward from high-level to low-level, starting with the business domain—that is, what changes in the business architecture are required to achieve the target vision. This will then illuminate what needs to transform in the data, applications, and finally, the technology domain. We will discuss this further in chapter 7, but it is important to go ahead and have the picture of this top-down approach in mind now.

Risk Assessment

In any approach being taken, there will always be risks involved. Change within an enterprise can always produce challenges and disruptions, which is why enterprises can sometimes be reluctant to change. In a sense, there is never an "ideal time" to implement changes, but failure to do so can have disastrous consequences for the enterprise.

So rather than waiting for the perfect timing for transformation to occur, enterprises need to have risk management tools in place that will help limit business disruption as much as possible. Any time there is a "business transformation risk," there are several risk management assessments and techniques that can be employed to analyze the situation on the front end of the EA process so that risks can be mitigated and transition plans put in place to address the known risks.

An enterprise may conduct some additional risk assessments continuously throughout the transformation as new information comes to light, but in general, as much as possible should be accomplished as early as possible. In that way, it is not a one-time activity but is ongoing so that the enterprise can remain proactive rather than reactive.

For example, on an Enterprise Level, we can think of Amazon's acquisition of Whole Foods and the type of risk analysis that would have been conducted for that particular merger.

In that analysis, they would ask questions like these:

- Is the acquisition of Whole Foods in line with Amazon's corporate vision and mission?

- If we move forward, how are we going to utilize Whole Foods with our other business units?

- Will this acquisition enhance our business? If so, how exactly?

- What internal factors will be impacted?

- What external factors will be impacted?

With the acquisition of Whole Foods, Amazon was taking on a fully functioning business with its own brand and customer base, unlike when they created businesses from the ground up like their Kindle platform. Therefore, the decision was not just rooted in "Can we do this?" They certainly had the resources to do so. Rather, the decision had to be based more around the questions "Should we do this?" and "How do we do this?"

From a customer view, the transition was fairly seamless. The shopping experience at Whole Foods is almost identical to before the acquisition, except now you can get a discount for scanning your Amazon Prime membership barcode.

But from the enterprise view, they had to examine everything from existing shipping relationships and existing business relationships with agricultural providers, to what HR policies and systems were already in place and needed transformation, to financial transaction services. Each of those aspects carried risks that needed to be assessed and planned for before any decision was made to acquire Whole Foods.

From an IT perspective of the Amazon–Whole Foods acquisition, Amazon had to develop an understanding of the existing landscape of Whole Foods and determine whether it was aligned with Amazon's existing landscape. What technological resources could be used to bring the two entities into alignment? What challenges would there be to integrate Whole Foods's IT landscape? This might include IT functions, from inventory management software to office applications like spreadsheets and word processing.

They also needed to consider how Whole Foods could support Amazon's existing business structures. For example, could Whole Foods locations be utilized as a shipping service to help customers more easily return unwanted items and therefore improve the customer experience?

Now once the analysis has been completed, the next step an enterprise will take is to develop and conduct some mitigation actions.

In the case of Southeast Regional Bank, one of the risks that was assessed was the potential for loss or misuse of customer data.

Since one of their goals was to develop a single view of the customer across the business units, this meant consolidating that information from across multiple databases and multiple software systems. With any kind of consolidation process and data migration from one system to another, there is always the risk of losing data, but there were also regulatory and legal concerns in regard to customer privacy.

So one of the mitigating actions they took to ensure they were abiding by privacy laws was to have their legal department study the regulations and then draft a statement that needed to be distributed to all of their customers across the business units, notifying them about the data transfer process and providing a way for customers to learn more if they wanted to.

Part of the function of an effective Enterprise Architect is to help the EA Board and EA Team with identifying the right risk management tools and dividing the potential risks into two classifications:

- Initial Risks: Those present prior to any mitigating actions

- Residual Risks: Those remaining after any mitigating actions

Dividing up these two types of risks creates clarity and also a more linear approach to addressing them. Different frameworks will have a variety of recommended risk assessments that can be utilized, which is where the reference frameworks we discussed in chapter 3 may come in handy, especially if you are in one of those industries.

For those utilizing TOGAF®, the Open Group utilizes a risk assessment known as Open FAIR (Factor Analysis of Information Risk). Oftentimes, the approach you take will dictate what risk assessment to utilize. Baseline First approaches will often have fewer risks since they are focused on incremental changes, whereas Target First approaches will often have more risks since they are focused on radical changes.

Conclusion

The architectural transformation for Southeast Regional Bank was one of those situations where both Target First and Baseline First approaches had to be used within different phases of the changes being implemented. Each carried risks with them that, once properly assessed, helped map out the actions that needed to be taken.

While Baseline First will be the most common you will encounter in your enterprise, it is key to know when to utilize a Target First approach since every industry goes through seasons of radical transformation brought about by innovation or disruptions in the marketplace. In fact, in the history of EA, from around 2000 to 2010, enterprises were rarely using Target First approaches because they were averse to going through radical changes in their enterprises. That is completely understandable, as you really only want to make radical changes when absolutely necessary, but to assume that your enterprise can adapt and innovate only through incremental Baseline First approaches can be a dangerous assumption over the long term.

For example, imagine you are part of a well-established, large enterprise in the Fortune 500. It is nothing for such an enterprise to have five thousand to ten thousand applications and technological assets being used within the scope of the business. Trying to make incremental changes to all of these pieces over the course of years without ever addressing the enterprise on a larger scale could be detrimental, as small problems compound into larger ones. By the time you collect a quarter of the data to identify the pain points on this number of applications, more marketplace or digital transformations will have occurred that will make that work moot.

Companies that attempt Baseline First approaches exclusively typically end up in a vicious cycle of collecting baseline information without any real transformation taking place, which ultimately means wasted time and resources because there was no value in the information that was collected. This leads to the EA process being seen as a waste and being abandoned altogether when any C-level officers (CXOs) view it as ineffective.

However, in reality, it was not the EA process that was ineffective—it was the approach and the lack of involvement of the stakeholders (that is, the users of those applications). Complex organizations require more complex approaches to effectively transform and innovate not only at a high level but also within every level of the enterprise. Not only did they fail to start in the correct place, but they also approached the problem from the wrong angle and without complete data to have a clear view of the problem.

Imagine you are the owner of a ten-story building, and you want to do a renovation, but instead of talking to the tenants of the building about the issues they see or hiring an inspection team, you try to do it all yourself. You would spend an enormous amount of time trying to document all of the items that need improvement, meaning the problems are only getting worse in that time, and you would probably still miss some of the issues that are problems for the tenants who are the primary stakeholders in that scenario.

This is why it's key to have members of every discipline within the enterprise contribute to the EA process. Without a clear understanding of the true pain points for the stakeholders, you could end up taking the wrong approach and not addressing the root issues. With data and information coming from all levels of the enterprise, you can better identify what areas require a Baseline First approach and when it may be necessary to do a more radical change through a Target First approach. In the next chapter, we will closely examine the various levels of architecture that will be approached and transformed so that you can begin to see how the approaches and frameworks work together in harmony to create your new blueprint.

CHAPTER TAKEAWAYS

▶ Taking the right approach for the right problem always yields better and faster results.

▶ Baseline First approaches are used for incremental changes, such as on a Process Level at which Six Sigma, Lean principles, or both can be implemented.

▶ Target First approaches are used for radical enterprise changes brought about by technological innovation or changes in the marketplace.

▶ Risk assessments are essential in the approach; risks should be assessed before implementing the architectural transformations to determine mitigation actions and should be assessed again after mitigation takes place.

▶ The approach you take will help determine what risk assessment needs to be conducted. Baseline First will tend to have fewer risks, whereas Target First will tend to have more risks.

▶ Information should be gathered directly from the stakeholders to help determine the scope of change that needs to occur and therefore the type of approach for the greatest chance of success.

CHAPTER 7

LEVELS OF ENTERPRISE ARCHITECTURE

One thing about being an Enterprise Architect is that it is certainly never boring. Every organization is different in structure, mission, and the problems they are facing, which makes every EA project a new challenge. Part of this is because, depending on which part of the organization someone belongs to, they will have a different perspective of the process.

Perhaps you have heard of the old analogy of three blind men being asked to describe an elephant. One examines the trunk and says, "This creature has very long, flexible limbs." Another examines the foot and says, "No, this creature has very heavy, large limbs." And the third examines the tail and says, "No, this creature has short, thin limbs with hair."

As I mentioned in the last chapter, this is why it is so essential for there to be input from stakeholders across the enterprise because CXOs will have one view of the enterprise, department directors will have another, and lower-level employees will have another.

Bringing all of these perspectives together, with input from every level, creates a fuller, more holistic picture of how the enterprise can be optimized.

CXOs will have one view of the enterprise, department directors will have another, and lower-level employees will have another.

Understanding the responsibilities and expectations of each level of the enterprise is helpful, though, since they must all work together for transformation to be successful. Before we can discuss the levels of EA, though, we first need to discuss architecture partitioning, which is a technique for dividing the architecture across four dimensions:

- Breadth: The number of business units to be impacted by the architectural transformation

- Depth: The level of detail required (Strategic, Segment, Project)

- Domains: Business, data, application, technology

- Time: Length of time needed to achieve the Target Architecture

Typically, this partitioning process will occur at the very beginning of the architecture initiative in order to better manage the pieces. The EA Board will play the lead role in the partitioning process, using the outputs as a guide for determining the approach and action steps with minimal risk.

With a big initiative like Southeast Regional Bank becoming a one-stop shop, the partitioning process was key in preventing the phases and implementation from becoming unmanageable or more cumbersome than necessary.

In their situation, the breadth was fairly simple to determine because *all* of their business units were being impacted. That may not be the case in your enterprise, especially if you're approaching a process Baseline First. The depth relates directly to everything we've already discussed with the levels of architecture within the enterprise and how high level or granular each initiative needs to be. The domains serve as a guide to ensure all aspects of the transformation are being covered within the EA process: How does the initiative transform the business? What data is being utilized? What applications are needed for optimization? And what technology will bring it all together?

And finally, what does the timeline look like for accomplishing the initiatives, and in what order do they need to happen? This goes back to the process of roadmapping and prioritizing the specific initiatives in a way that will mitigate risks and make the process more efficient without sacrificing quality.

A good analogy for this process is to think of it a bit like city planning. The city planner doesn't usually plan out the entire city, after all, but instead divides the city up into distinct zones: industrial, residential, commercial, and so on. Likewise, you can think of architecture partitioning as the "zoning" process for the enterprise, in which you classify and divide along the aforementioned factors in order to simplify the process and create clarity from the complexity.

The important thing to keep in mind with partitioning is that it should be based on the desired end state, not on the baseline. At the end of the day, though, no matter how large or complex the enterprise, no matter how the architecture is partitioned, there are three levels to Enterprise Architecture:

- Strategic (Enterprise Level)

- Segment (Program or Portfolio Level)

- Project (Capability Level)

Enterprise Architecture Board (CXO, EA, SME)		
Segment Architecture Board (BUH, DIR, SegA, DA, PA, IA)	Segment Architecture Board (BUH, DIR, SegA, DA, PA, IA)	Segment Architecture Board (BUH, DIR, SegA, DA, PA, IA)

Implementation Projects

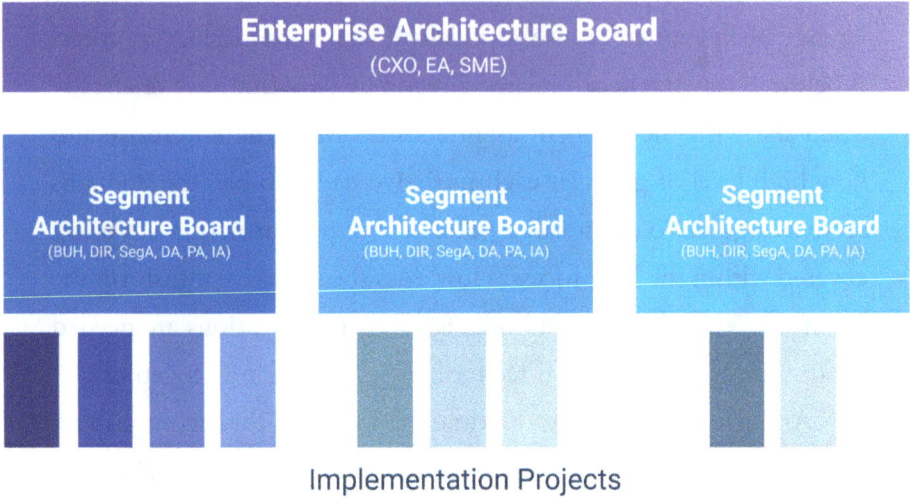

When helping Southeast Regional Bank with their EA transformation, the CXOs had the goal of transforming the business into a one-stop shop for banking, but this would have significant and varying ramifications for their employees in commercial banking, loans, insurance, and so on.

So it is essential to not think of only one level of their enterprise but to consider all levels involved, no matter what framework or approach is being utilized, as different requirements will impact different levels. Also, actions taken at the Strategic Level will have ramifications for the Segment and Project Levels, while actions on the Project Level will have ramifications for the Segment and Strategic Levels.

In fact, one of the simplest ways to think of it is that the enterprise works from high-level (strategic) architecture down to low-level architecture (project), and the outputs of each level will become the inputs of the level below it. In this way, one level of transformation informs and impacts another seamlessly rather than being siloed.

When enterprises attempt to perform architecture transformation at separate levels without inputs flowing from one to the other, it results in not only a disjointed process but also inefficiency and poor communication.

If the enterprise is utilizing the TOGAF® framework, then each level will be taken through the ADM process to ensure all four domains are fully considered and optimized. This necessitates some level of repetition, but that is a strength of this approach because the process of repetition is exactly what allows problems to be fully identified, addressed, and optimized.

You could compare it to the process of a film director watching the day's footage or "dailies" over and over along with the film editor, identifying the best elements and cutting away the problem areas to create the best film possible. In that situation, they also start out at the high level and work to low level, as follows:

High-Level/Strategic: What kind of film are we wanting to make? Genre, tone, storyline, etc.

Midlevel/Segment: What are the scenes that the film is made up of? Which ones support the overall vision of the film and which ones need to be cut? Character plotlines, locations, etc.

Low-Level/Capability: What is needed to make these scenes the best? Editing, selection of the best takes, costumes, set design, equipment, etc.

No one level is more important than another, but they work together. Shoddy costume design at the low level could create a poor film reception at the high level when it's reviewed by critics. Rather, all levels need to inform one another and work within a unified vision

Strategic Architecture

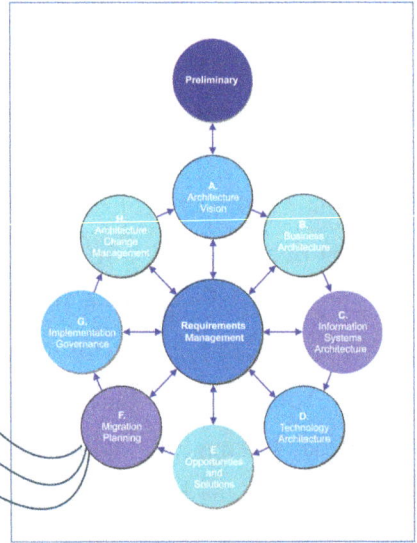

Segment Architecture

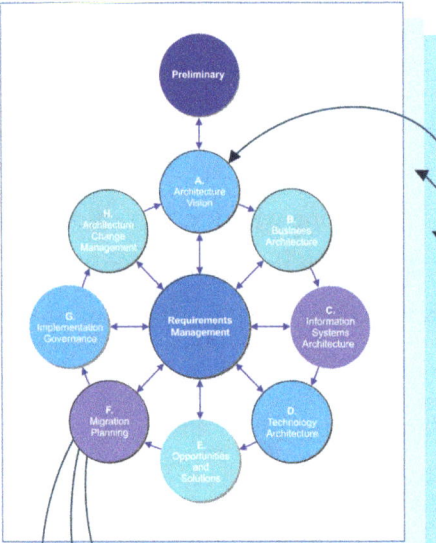

Capability Architecture

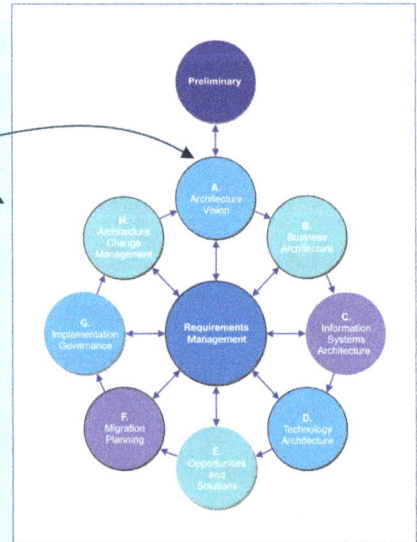

to make an exceptional film that will perform well at the box office and receive good reviews for long-term impact. Likewise, TOGAF® assists an enterprise into breaking down these components, performing the necessary repetitions and iterations that will help the enterprise become the best possible version of itself.

Now to get a better idea of what this looks like practically in the context of going through an entire TOGAF® EA process, we will walk through it together level by level, combining the elements you learned in chapters 4 and 5 to show how the ADM helps identify the necessary actions that need to be taken that will optimize the enterprise. In many ways, this will be the "main course" of our entire EA discussion. While this makes this particular chapter lengthy, I believe it's important to see how each of these concepts we've discussed so far interacts and informs the others at each level of the enterprise.

Strategic/Enterprise Level

Strategic architecture takes an enterprise high-level view, developing the strategies for the entire organization. Whether it is a business or technology strategy, this level seeks to understand the drivers behind the strategic architecture and then identify the high-level initiatives the enterprise needs to take on to fulfill those strategies.

The EA Board and Enterprise Architects will be involved at this level of architecture, including any C-Suite members included in the EA Board. Drivers can be brainstormed many ways, but it is essential they include many perspectives, as we discussed in the last chapter. For example, if the CEO is leading the initiative, they may conduct workshops with the stakeholders to determine some pain points to discover what the key drivers are.

Let's say that an enterprise is undergoing a digital transformation through replacing older technology with newer applications. There are three primary steps that it must go through:

- First, there must be an understanding of the drivers for the strategy, why it's being done, and what it's going to accomplish—that is, how it is going to improve the enterprise.

- Second, they have to identify the initiatives that can come out of the digital transformation.

- Finally, a high-level roadmap of those initiatives is developed to determine how they can be implemented in the Strategic-Level architecture.

Now drivers may be internal or external. The easiest way to understand the difference between the two is that internal drivers are those that are under the direct control of the enterprise, whereas external are those outside of your direct control. External drivers could include such things as laws and regulations, changes in the market, vendor management, or tools and products being purchased by the company. Internal drivers could be things like consolidating tech infrastructure, business model integration, or digital transformation.

From the drivers, you then develop a list of enablers—that is, the initiatives or solutions that enable the drivers. For example, if the primary business driver is "to increase profit," then there are some specific ways that can be enabled—an enterprise can increase the business by adding products or services, or they can decrease costs through eliminating inefficiencies.

If they decide to increase the business, perhaps they do so by producing a new product or creating some new channels for marketing, such as social media campaigns, or developing some methods to cross-sell products to existing customers with their MDM (Master Data Management) or CRM solutions.

To return to the example of Southeast Regional Bank, one of their major drivers included their need for improving financial reporting across all business units. The understanding of this strategy was obvious enough—with more timely and efficient financial reports, the business could have a clearer picture of revenue, which meant that they could also be more responsive to potential problems, whether they came from within the enterprise or were caused by the market.

With that understanding, they identified several initiatives for streamlining financial reporting, including building a catalog of each business unit's reporting procedures and processes, what software—if any—was being used, and how that information was being consolidated at the Corporate Level.

From that catalog of initiatives, they constructed their high-level roadmap of what order these initiatives should be completed in and how they should connect with one another for the achieved end. Now perhaps they found in the second step that their insurance business unit had the most efficient reporting method, and they decided to use it as the standard for the other units to align with. One by one, they will work with each business unit, updating their reporting process until the desired target state has been achieved.

Now let's see how this plays out side by side with the ADM and how the process is tailored at each level of the enterprise throughout the process.

PRELIMINARY PHASE

In this opening phase of the ADM, the focus is on preparation and initiation activities for creating the Architecture Capability. In terms of the Enterprise Level, the inputs will primarily be the strategic business drivers but will also include any other existing factors at the start of the EA process, such as board strategies, business plans, legal frameworks, existing partnerships, or contractual agreements. There must be a high-level assessment of the enterprise organizational model and framework "as is" in order to get a grasp of where the problem areas are.

At the Strategic Level, these should reflect the greatest concerns of the enterprise that are prompting the need for EA change. In fact, the Preliminary Phase often involves revisiting the enterprise's mission statement since they are looking at their long-term goals over the next twenty or thirty years. To keep it simple here, we will focus on the ultimate goal of Southeast Regional Bank to transform into a "one-stop shop for banking."

> There must be a high-level assessment of the enterprise organizational model and framework "as is" in order to get a grasp of where the problem areas are.

In order to do this, they had to first define their current state and what was preventing them from becoming a one-stop shop for banking. These could be summarized as follows:

- No enterprise-wide strategy
- Financial reports six months out of date
- No single view of the customer
- No management control
- No one architectural approach

These concerns then drive the Enterprise Architect to scope the enterprise, meaning they will ask: "*Which organizations within the enterprise will be impacted?*"

While this would not be the case for every enterprise, in the situation facing Southeast Regional Bank, becoming a one-stop banking shop would impact *all* organizations within the enterprise, so at the Strategic Level, that included the following:

- Retail Bank

- Corporate Bank

- Insurance and Investments Unit

- Loans Unit

- External Credit Card Partners

The Preliminary Phase especially lends itself to the Strategic Level since it will further define the governance and supporting frameworks that will manage the EA process, including setting up the Architecture Board and identifying who has the necessary skills to be on the EA Team at all three levels.

Once the EA Team is established, they will select an EA tool, which will act as a repository for keeping up with all of the information that is being gathered at every level of the process. In addition to this, Architecture Principles will be established that align with the drivers.

As previously mentioned, these principles will help form the "rule book" of how decisions will be made at the Segment and Capabilities Level. Becoming a one-stop shop for banking will inevitably create some disruption, so to prevent you from having to flip back to chapter 6, here is the example principle for "Business Continuity":

PRINCIPLE	Business Continuity
STATEMENT	The operations of all business units within Southeast Regional Bank will be maintained even in the event of any disruptions to the system.
RATIONALE	The key stakeholders in applying technology to meet business needs are any information users within Southeast Regional Bank, such as employees, but can also include customers accessing their private information. To ensure that information management is synced within the enterprise, it is essential that every organization in the enterprise be involved in every element of the information environment. Business experts from each segment of the enterprise need to team up with the technical staff tasked with the development and maintenance of the information environment with the objective of defining the goals of IT.
IMPLICATIONS	To function as a team, each stakeholder must take responsibility for the development of the information environment. Implementation of this principle will require resources.

At the Strategic Level, these principles will closely align with the drivers and objectives prompting the EA process. At the end of the day, they exist to help organizations make decisions and provide "guide rails" to the process throughout.

From there, the framework is tailored for the client's needs, so in the case of Southeast Regional Bank, this is where we knew we would need to integrate the BIAN framework along with TOGAF®. Were it a retail operation, we would tailor it with ARTS; if telecom, we would tailor it with Frameworx; and so on, as we discussed in chapter 3. As you might recall from chapter 5, it's also typical at this stage to tailor terminology within the enterprise so that everyone involved is "speaking the same language" to reduce any confusion in the process.

Tailoring of the ADM will happen at every level, but at the Strategic Level, it might mean looking deeper into the business motivations of the enterprise and gaining a better understanding of the goals and mission with more detail.

At this point, the Enterprise Architect and EA Team will develop a strategy for addressing the needs of the enterprise's stakeholders, whether those are the C-Suite, the customers, employees, vendors, or whoever else may be impacted by the initiative. The EA tools (e.g., HOPEX, ARIS, Alfabet, or others listed in chapter 5 on page 92) will also be selected, which will empower the stakeholders for quick and effective decision making throughout the process.

Even here at the Strategic Level, you can see how each of the four domains is taken into consideration for impact and transformation:

- Business (Drivers, partnerships, legal requirements)

- Data (Repository selection)

- Application (EA tools selected)

- Technology (Tech being utilized in reference frameworks)

Beyond that, the Preliminary Phase provides the Strategic-Level view of the desired organizational model for the Enterprise Architecture, the governance framework, a tailored framework that will impact each level of the structure, and a tailored catalog of Architecture Principles that will guide decisions at each level.

A. VISION PHASE

The outputs from the Preliminary Phase become the inputs for the Vision Phase, which establishes the scope of the EA, identifies the stakeholders, and creates the Architecture Vision, which simply defines what the desired outcome for the architecture should be. This vision must be decided from the very beginning so that there is consistency and singular purpose throughout the many stages of the process. The other objective of this phase is gaining approval for the Statement of Architecture Work, which outlines the necessary programs and processes that will fulfill the vision.

At the Strategic Level, the first step is to establish the EA project by gaining top-level management buy-in, ensuring that the Architecture Vision is consistent with the needs of the enterprise. Therefore, if the vision in our case study is "becoming a one-stop shop for banking," then the main question must be "Is the board in accord with taking the necessary steps to make that happen?" These changes will cause disruption, so having the full support from management will help make sure things keep moving in the direction of optimization.

Let me take a moment to assure you that this is not repeating the steps taken in the Preliminary Phase but is actually *confirming* those steps. The Vision Phase is dedicated to further clarifying who will be most impacted enterprise-wide and confirming the goals, drivers, and constraints in a checks-and-balances methodology. After all, there may be new goals and drivers identified that were not initially thought of during the preparation stage. Perhaps there are new constraints, such as state or federal laws, budgetary adjustments, and so on that enter the picture now that the process has actually begun. It is better to have those clearly identified here at the highest level than at the Segment or Capability Level, when it may be too late to course-correct.

Furthermore, the Vision Phase evaluates the enterprise's capabilities at a high level and assesses the readiness of the business to undergo transformation. This includes defining the scope of the EA, considering the breadth (number of business units that will be impacted), the depth (level of detail required), ensuring that all four architecture domains will be considered, and the timeline for achieving the Target

Architecture. Again, this is not repetition of the Preliminary Phase but checking and confirming it.

A note on considering all the domains: You may recall from earlier in the book, that during the Enterprise Architecture 2.0 Phase of the early 2000s, often the technology domain was the driving force behind enterprise transformations based on the latest, greatest tech. The problem with such an approach is that then, tech was informing the business vision when it should have been the other way around. Since technology is always changing, you want to ensure that the long-term business vision remains the guiding force.

The Vision Phase evaluates the enterprise's capabilities at a high level and assesses the readiness of the business to undergo transformation.

From there, the Vision Phase will also elaborate and confirm the principles from the Preliminary Phase to make sure they support the vision and that there is agreement and clear direction on the Enterprise Level. This will help bring further clarity to the Architecture Vision and define the target value propositions through specific KPIs, which will measure the effectiveness of the EA transformation.

As mentioned before, there will be disruption with any change to the architecture, so a risk management plan will be developed to look at the big picture of how the transformation could impact the enterprise. Finally, this will lead to a Statement of Architecture Work requiring the Architecture Board's approval.

B. BUSINESS ARCHITECTURE PHASE

In this phase of the ADM at the Strategic Level, the primary objectives are to establish a plan for how to get the enterprise from its

Baseline Architecture (point A) to its Target Architecture (point B). Rather than performing business architecture at this level, the focus is more on defining the business strategy for the entire enterprise and how to start addressing the concerns. To do this, a gap analysis will be conducted to find what is missing and to develop an Architecture Roadmap of specific steps to follow.

Now these specific steps will be broken up into segments and then capabilities in the lower levels, but here this is where the roadmap components are defined that will help clarify what needs to happen between point A and point B. In terms of the four domains, the gap analysis will help illuminate not only the gaps in the business architecture but also in the data, application, and technology architectures. Additionally, there is an impact analysis that will help look at what the wider implications are for the business, such as any preexisting architectures.

As such, this phase is designed to look primarily at the business domain and create the plan—or roadmap, rather—for accomplishing this.

Example:

Baseline—What is preventing Southeast Regional Bank from becoming a one-stop shop for banking? How is the current structure of the enterprise negatively impacting the business in terms of revenue and remaining competitive in the marketplace?

Target—What is the overall business benefit of becoming a one-stop shop for banking? How would it help us better care for our customers to create more customer loyalty? How would it be better for employees, shareholders, and the other stakeholders?

All of this information will then be reviewed to ensure the concerns are being appropriately addressed and then finalize the business architecture to be achieved by the transformation.

C. INFORMATION SYSTEMS ARCHITECTURE PHASE (DATA AND APPLICATIONS)

You may recall from chapter 4, it was mentioned that in tailoring the ADM to the enterprise, there may be phases of the ADM that are not needed. At the Strategic Level, we typically skip over the Information Systems Phase, as it will play a much greater role at the Segment Level. At the Segment Level, it will actually be separated into two pieces, one looking at the domain of data and the other looking at the applications domain.

D. TECHNOLOGY ARCHITECTURE PHASE

Just like in the Business Architecture Phase, a roadmap must be established that defines the Baseline and Target Architectures for the enterprise to be optimized. It's important to emphasize that the specific actions of the roadmap are not taken here at the Strategic Level but are simply defined to establish exactly what work needs to be done. In other words, the technology solutions themselves will not be decided upon, but the enterprise will lay out a strategic view of where they want to be and the guiding principles for the role of technology throughout the enterprise.

The strategic view of the target technology architecture can be looked at as the "big picture" view, taking the Vision Phase view of "Where do we want to be in thirty years?" and applying this to the technology domain, setting into motion the processes and tools that will help the enterprise adapt to new technology over the next thirty years.

For example, the board could say, "To remain competitive and become a one-stop shop, we need to move toward utilizing cloud computing." They will not pick the specific cloud-based architectures but rather lay out the strategy that will then empower the decision making that will occur during this same phase at the Segment Level.

E. OPPORTUNITIES AND SOLUTIONS PHASE

At a high level, this phase facilitates a strategic view of all the opportunities and solutions available to the enterprise so that decisions can be made, consolidating the information from the previous phases. More specifically, the solutions are the enablers that are paired with the drivers.

Again, rather than selecting the specific solution, it is framed around the strategic vision, such as: "In order to become a one-stop shop, we need to develop opportunities to cross-sell our products to existing customers." With that view, an implementation and migration strategy is developed, which will inform what the exact segments will be at the Segment Level. Typically such a plan focuses first on the "low-hanging fruit," then moves toward achievable targets along an established timeline from the present state to the optimized state.

F. MIGRATION PLANNING PHASE

As its name implies, this phase is focused on the transformation process both by finalizing the Architecture Roadmap along with an implementation and migration plan. As shown in the last diagram (page 134), this phase is of particular note, as the outputs of this phase will provide the inputs for the Segment Level's Vision Phase.

To become a one-stop shop for banking, Southeast Regional Bank defined a list of objectives (segments) to take them from the Baseline to Target Architectures as follows:

- Create enterprise-wide business strategy

- Create a single view of the customer

- Improve financial reporting

- Consolidation of physical assets

With these segments identified, the EA Board will complete the implementation and migration plan, which lays out how the enterprise will move from baseline to target states and refine the desired timeline. This phase also provides an opportunity to complete the strategic view of the architecture development cycle and document what lessons were learned that could apply to the next cycle.

G. IMPLEMENTATION GOVERNANCE PHASE

This phase serves as a type of review of the previous phase and confirming necessary governance for undergoing transformation. From a strategic view, the EA Board will confirm the scope and priorities for the deployment of new solutions as they are selected at the lower levels, identify resources for deployment, and conduct a compliance review to catch any errors or verify that standards are being met.

At the Strategic Level, governance will provide the permission and resources for implementing the business and IT operations transformation (which will occur in the lower levels) and then conduct the necessary postimplementation reviews to close out the implementation process.

H. ARCHITECTURE CHANGE MANAGEMENT PHASE

This phase is focused on maintaining the architecture life cycle, confirming that the governance framework is executed, ensuring that the transformation will fulfill the requirements that were set out by the vision, and formalizing a plan for future cycles.

This is accomplished by establishing a value realization process, setting up some monitoring tools that will facilitate continuous feedback, managing ongoing risks, providing analysis (typically through service level agreements), and developing requirements of when another cycle needs to begin. Once all of these items are established, then the EA Board can activate the process to actually begin the transformation.

REQUIREMENTS MANAGEMENT

You may recall from the ADM diagram that Requirements Management is not a phase of the ADM but rather sits at the center of all of these phases as an essential part of managing the many requirements that are identified within each phase that may also impact the other phases. It provides the means for documenting and monitoring the various baseline requirements and identifying those that need to be changed during the ADM.

This provides a good check-and-balance that each of the four domains are being considered and returns focus to the Architecture Vision. It also enables the ongoing impact assessments of any changes and the necessary requirements for implementing the changes. In many ways, it is like the hub holding the spokes of the wheel in place, allowing the machine to move forward. While the requirements management is present at each of the three levels, I will only mention it here since it plays exactly the same role in both the Segment and Project Levels, serving as a type of "glue" between the three levels.

But now it's time to turn our attention to the Segment-Level architecture and how each of these phases are tailored there.

Segment/Program/Portfolio Level

Even though the Segment Level is "lower" than the Enterprise Level, it actually has a higher level of detail since it is focused upon identifying the details of the high-level roadmap established in the Strategic Level. Here, the architecture looks at aspects like the applications, data, and infrastructures needed to implement the strategic initiatives. As noted in the diagram on page 97, there may be a Segment Architecture Board set up to make key decisions at the Segment Level, take instructions from the EA Team, and gain the approval of the EA Board. This group may be populated by business unit heads, segment heads, or domain architects working at the Segment Level.

You may recall that another one of Southeast Regional Bank's Strategic-Level concerns was recognizing they had no single view of the customer. This concern translates into a Segment-Level driver that can be summarized as "Create a single view of the customer." This will be further segmented into the initiatives—or Work Packages—that will provide the inputs for the Capability Level.

Now it's important to emphasize here that the Segment Level does not always pertain to a specific business unit alone. Often a segment, program, or portfolio will cross over multiple business units; therefore, it's essential to have a clear understanding of the implications and impact the transformations will make. For example, if the program that needs to be architected is "Customer Service," that is a segment that does not belong to a single business unit but applies across most of the business units in some capacity.

At other times, a segment may be designated to a specific business

> The Segment Level does not always pertain to a specific business unit alone.

unit if the Enterprise-Level driver identified it as so. For example, this could happen if an enterprise just acquired a new business unit and is taking a Baseline First approach to integrate the new business into the enterprise through incremental changes. In a case like that, the segment architecture could be isolated to the new business unit alone if solutions are already optimized across the other existing business units.

Each one of these identified segments must then be architected, utilizing the nine phases of the ADM to determine the specific ways those segments can be optimized. We skip the Preliminary Phase at the Segment Level since it really only pertains to setting the stage for the Strategic/Enterprise Level.

Now let's take a closer look at how this applied to Southeast Regional Bank in terms of their segment initiatives. Based on the concerns/drivers they identified for architecture transformation, the implementation and migration plan outlined the direction of the transformation as follows:

- No enterprise-wide strategy (baseline) to enterprise-wide strategy (target)

- Financial reports six months out of date (baseline) to up-to-date financial reports (target)

- No single view of the customer (baseline) to single view of the customer (target)

To keep this simple, however, we're going to zero in on their goal to streamline and improve their financial reporting across all of their business units. Let's imagine for a moment that part of the problem with their financial reporting was that each business unit was using its own accounting software and that, due to mergers and acquisitions over time, some units start their Q1 on January 1, while others mark their Q1 on July 1. You can imagine the confusion that would lead to.

Adhering to the principles that were established in the Strategic Level, the Segment-Level goal might also include looking at consolidating infrastructure across the enterprise, such as the specific applications being used for financial accounting and reporting and how consolidation will benefit Business Continuity in the long term.

A. VISION PHASE

Just like at the Enterprise Level, there has to be buy-in from the governance for the segments that have been identified. Since the EA Team will be made up of an assortment of all the business units needed for streamlining the financial reporting, there will be requirements laid out such as budget constraints and identification of what current solutions are being utilized as well as a reiteration of the stakeholder concerns at the Segment Level, since there may be a more detailed view of those concerns than what exists at the Strategic Level.

There will then be an assessment of the readiness for the transformation to occur in the identified segment with similar scoping of the EA, considering the business units to be impacted by transforming the financial reporting and confirming that all four architecture domains are considered. These units may be identified in the following areas:

- Finance department (business)

- Customer management system (data)

- Accounting software (applications)

- Cloud computing (technology)

You'll notice that all of these capabilities fit into the overall strategic vision of becoming the "one-stop banking shop" and helping the enterprise along the road to accomplish that strategic vision. Furthermore, there may be additional principles laid out to further clarify the goal of the program and define its value to the business. Once established, these will require approval before the capabilities identified can be acted upon at the Capability/Project Level.

B. BUSINESS ARCHITECTURE PHASE

At the Segment Level, this phase focuses on getting the programs from the Baseline to Target Architectures. Like with the Strategic Level, a gap analysis is conducted, but it will be centered on the specific segments identified to define the value proposition of the transformation, build the roadmap, and conduct an impact analysis assessing the preexisting architectures. The EA Team can then begin to plan out exactly how they will streamline financial reporting across all business units.

Example:

Baseline—Why is financial reporting currently six months behind? How is this impacting the revenue of the business in terms of shareholders, employees, and customers?

Target—What is the overall business benefit of better financial reporting? What new services could we identify with better reporting that would help spur revenue generation? How can we provide more value to customers to generate more customer loyalty? How can we make the work better for employees to reduce staff burnout and turnover costs?

C. PART 1: INFORMATION SYSTEMS (DATA) ARCHITECTURE PHASE

Similar to how the previous phase identified the start and finish lines for the business domain, so this phase shifts its focus to the data domain. This phase will help enable both the business architecture and Architecture Vision. From a Segment-Level view, a similar gap analysis and impact analysis are conducted to help define the roadmap of how to get the data architecture to where it needs to be.

During this phase of the Segment Level, the EA Team is collecting the necessary data to have a clear understanding of the current data architecture. They will follow the same steps that were followed at the Enterprise Level but with more detail and focus on the assigned segment they are responsible for. Information will be collected from all of the pertinent business units to identify the candidate components for the segment roadmap. With Southeast Regional Bank, this was quite an undertaking because, in helping them improve their financial reporting (Architecture Vision), it was revealed that this would include not only the finance data itself but also employee data and customer data.

Example:

Baseline—What data do we currently have available to work with? What data is already being reported across the business units?

Target—What data is needed for better long-term financial reporting? What data needs to be reported across business units, and how is it going to be accounted for?

C. PART 2: INFORMATION SYSTEMS (APPLICATIONS) ARCHITECTURE PHASE

This phase at the Segment Level is, again, very similar in its process to the previous one but is designed to consider the applications that are being used in terms of the data that was identified. Therefore, there is an analysis of what applications are in use across the enterprise, which will help identify any gaps or redundancies that need to be addressed at the Segment Level to benefit the entire enterprise.

Even at the Segment Level, there is no selection of the applications themselves, as those will be determined at the Capability Level. Rather, the EA Board will be looking at what is currently in use across the enterprise, from the applications themselves to the policies and principles connected with those applications. From there, they can put together a holistic strategy for how applications should be selected and utilized throughout the enterprise in a way that will best satisfy the business and vision architectures. By identifying the needs that the applications at the Segment Level must fulfill, the EA Team can begin the process of composing the segment roadmap.

Example:

Baseline—What applications are currently being used for data management and financial reporting across the business units?

Target—How will we streamline the applications in use to ensure no loss in data communication and improve financial reporting? What will the applications-approval process look like moving forward?

D. TECHNOLOGY ARCHITECTURE PHASE

By now you probably see the pattern emerging, but this phase turns its attention to looking at the segment requirements for technology. Equipped with the segment view of the business, data, and application domains, the enterprise can then create its strategy around the defined optimal state of its technology infrastructure, which will support the other domains already discussed.

This phase will identify the gaps in technology as well as what the impact of improving the infrastructure will be. Impacts could be negative or positive, after all. A positive impact could be improving the usability of applications by the employees through network upgrades. A negative impact could be that systems are inaccessible by customers for a window of time during the updates affecting the Business Continuity.

Example:

Baseline—How are financial services applications currently being enabled? What does the technology infrastructure and network health look like? What physical or legal standards are in place that we have to work within?

Target—What technology infrastructure needs improvement? What can be standardized across the enterprise? What will be the long-term plan for technology updates moving forward?

E. OPPORTUNITIES AND SOLUTIONS PHASE

With the information gathered from all four domains, this phase shifts gears to consolidate and analyze everything collected at the Segment Level to create a completed version of the roadmap. During the previous four phases, any phase may need to be revisited to reveal all the potential opportunities. For example, a gap identified in the technology infrastructure could prompt a revelation in the applications phase or data phase that needs another review.

This necessitates defining the Solutions Building Blocks (SBBs), which finalizes the view of the Target Architecture initially put forward in the Vision Phase. By consolidating everything, the enterprise can form a more simplified view not only of what gaps exist but also what constraints exist that could obstruct optimizations, what requirements exist across the domains, and what is needed for the reconciliation of interoperability. Furthermore, this phase validates and refines the enterprise's dependencies—that is, what components or processes need to be dealt with first for success while also confirming the readiness and risk for the business transformation to begin.

At the Segment Level, this phase creates a more formalized version of the roadmap, as it will identify the Work Packages to be performed at the Capability Level, along with what transition architectures may be required to ensure Business Continuity while the necessary transformations are taking place.

Just like at the Strategic Level, an implementation and migration strategy is developed for the segment of focus, starting with the "low-hanging fruit," and defined Work Packages are established. Therefore, if the segment is "improved financial reporting," the decision may be to start with the MDM because it contains most of the relevant data and has the most direct impact on customer experience.

F. MIGRATION PLANNING PHASE

At the Segment Level, this phase finalizes the Architecture Roadmap for the program initiative along with an implementation and migration plan, including a cost analysis. This analysis looks at the business value of the transformation in comparison to the cost of the Work Packages identified in the last phase.

This includes looking at how the completion of each Work Package will impact and interact with the others. The cost/benefit assessment allows more clarity on prioritizing each Work Package through conducting both a risk validation and business value assessment. Doing so will confirm the final components and structure of the Architecture Roadmap, which provides the inputs for the Vision Phase at the Capability Level. Streamlining the financial reporting then can be broken down into the following capabilities:

- Identification of data sources and entities
- Selection of new MDM
- Selection of new CRM
- Transition to cloud-based database
- Updating of reporting policies and procedures

Like at the Strategy Level, there will be documentation completed about what was learned that could help inform other segments to be architected or the next cycle of transformation.

G. IMPLEMENTATION GOVERNANCE PHASE

At the Segment Level, this phase serves as review of the Migration Planning Phase to ensure that it is aligned with the Strategic-Level vision's Target Architecture. Specifically, this includes confirming the alignment with the standards and principles through an EA compliance review and then identifying the necessary deployment resources to satisfy those criteria. Touch points are established between the Enterprise Architect and the operations team, and then approval will be sought for implementation via change requests detailing the transformations needed to achieve the Target Architecture.

H. ARCHITECTURE CHANGE MANAGEMENT PHASE

At the Segment Level, the roadmap for the segment initiative has been completed and will outline the specific capabilities to be architected at the Project Level. Like the Strategic Level, it will also look at maintaining the architecture life cycle, confirming that the governance framework is executed, and ensuring that the segment changes to be made will be aligned with the EA's requirements. There will be specific monitoring tools or practices defined for the assigned segment so that risks can be managed, and feedback can be available throughout the implementation that occurs at the Project Level.

Project/Capability Level

In the same way that the Enterprise-Level decisions cascaded into the Segment Level, so the Segment Level cascades into the Project- or Capability-Level architecture. As with the Migration Planning Phase at the Enterprise Level, the outputs of the Migration Planning Phase at the Segment Level form the capabilities to be architected at the Project/Capability Level. Therefore, this level discusses some of the implementations on a more granular level, the specific projects that must be undertaken in order for transformation and optimization to occur, which will impact all three levels.

In a sense, this level can be seen as the "task list" in the EA process, with specific projects that will be completed in order to transform the architecture. Southeast Regional Bank, at the Segment Level, identified several capabilities that needed to be addressed in order for them to improve their financial reporting, including standardizing and updating their MDM and CRM solutions. Each of those will be an individual capability that will inevitably involve a series of steps to fulfill them.

Throughout the ADM process at the Capability Levels, these action steps will be reviewed for approval to ensure that they are following the Architecture Principles and as part of the checks and balances of the EA process. Now let's say an enterprise is pursuing digital transformation at the Enterprise Level; then digital marketing strategy could be identified as a need at the Segment Level, and then a social media campaign could be implemented by the marketing department at the Project Level. That project will be assigned for completion to the marketing employees with the right skills to conduct it.

Practically speaking, a social media manager may be tasked with syncing up the timing of ads and optimizing SEO solutions while a graphic designer creates the ads that will be used in the campaign. In the same way that the process cascades down, the work done at the Project Level will then "cascade up" for review to the Segment Level and then to the Enterprise Level for final approval prior to implementation. As these tasks are conducted, approved, and completed, the architecture will be methodically transformed until it reaches its target state.

Now let's look at how the Project Level interacts with the nine phases of the ADM. Again, while many of the phases themselves are repeated, it will look different here and can sometimes prompt revisiting phases at either the Strategic or Segment Levels if new information or problems come to light. For simplicity, we will focus on the previous example from the Segment Level of consolidating data management through the selection and implementation of a new MDM.

A. VISION PHASE

At the Project Level, we take the outputs discovered at the Segment Level and break them into logical pieces by isolating actionable areas of the architecture transformation. In establishing a new MDM, the vision will begin to lay out what must happen before implementing the architectural transformation and how that fulfills the goals from the Segment Level. In this case, it can be as simple as saying, "Updating our MDM will allow the enterprise to accomplish better financial reporting."

It's important to note here that sometimes the project being worked on may also impact other segments. For example, updating the MDM will be essential for improving financial reporting, but it will also be instrumental in enabling the cross-selling of products, which was another segment identified during their Segment-Level Vision Phase.

So here it's important to remain focused on how the project vision will help accomplish the vision at the higher levels and to look specifically at the goals, drivers, and constraints of the project. Defining the scope of the project at the Capability Level means starting to outline the steps of the project. In the case of updating the MDM, it might look something like this:

- Upgrading of technology at identified business units

- Consolidation of the data into transition system

- Removal of redundancies of data within the system

- Review of missing data that did not migrate

- Performance of system checks and additional upgrades

- Upgrading of cybersecurity systems across the enterprise

- Launch of the new MDM

- Migration of data from transition system into the new MDM

Like at the previous levels, there must be support from the governance of this plan so there is assurance that this meets the needs of both the Segment- and Strategic-Level visions and addresses the stakeholder concerns at each of those levels. Even at the Project Level, the established Architecture Principles are applied to how the project should be conducted. Likewise, there will then be a readiness assessment prior to implementation and confirmation that all the domains are considered.

B. BUSINESS ARCHITECTURE PHASE

At the Project Level, this phase focuses on getting the assigned project from the Baseline to Target Architectures by looking at the results of a gap analysis and assessing the value of the project to the business. Ultimately, the phase assesses how the project will optimize the business architecture and fit into the Segment- and Strategic-Level goals that were established.

While different projects may be assigned to different individuals for the actual implementation, here, it is looking at how each of the project's action steps fits into the "big picture" and starts prioritizing them to develop the project roadmap. Even if some of the projects will be completed in the same timeframe, there may be ones that have to occur in a specific order for the greatest business value.

So one might look at the list of steps laid out in the Project Vision Phase and say, "It makes sense for us to review whether any data failed to migrate before we look for redundancies in the data. Redundancies can always be removed over time, but missing data could cause us lost revenue or costly communication issues." Oftentimes, there may be a logical order that must take place, such as "A" must be completed before "B" can be acted upon.

C. PART 1: INFORMATION SYSTEMS (DATA) ARCHITECTURE PHASE

Each project will have its own data that has to be assessed and analyzed, no matter what segment it belongs to. For example, the EA Team member tasked with consolidating all of the employee data across the enterprise will build a roadmap for how to reach the Target Architecture for their project.

Each project will have its own data that has to be assessed and analyzed, no matter what segment it belongs to.

They will do so by looking across all of the impacted business units identified in the Vision Phase of their project, looking at the baseline of where they are now and defining the steps that need to occur for the data to all be consolidated within a transition architecture. If a different member of the EA Team is tasked with the project of selecting the new MDM, they will need to coordinate with that team member to ensure consistency in how the data is to be managed as part of the requirements management.

C. PART 2: INFORMATION SYSTEMS (APPLICATIONS) ARCHITECTURE PHASE

Likewise, this phase will look at the applications in use that directly correlate to the assigned project or capability and identify the components of the roadmap for how to close the gap between the existing architectures to the target ones. In regard to the project of consolidating data, perhaps it is discovered that one business unit has stored employee data in a cloud-based database, another has stored employee data on a localized spreadsheet, and yet another is using an outdated database software. The EA Team member may compare their findings with those from the Segment Level to ensure that nothing is being missed.

Meanwhile, in the MDM project, the gap analysis could reveal that of the nine business units to be impacted by creating a single view of the customer, three of them are using one type of MDM system but without any communication between their localized versions, another three use a different MDM system, and the remaining three have their own system they are using. They might discover that five of the units are utilizing a cloud-based CRM, but only three of those five are sharing that system, and the other four are using localized CRMs.

In both of these projects, the team members will identify the applications that will enable them to close those gaps and fulfill their respective project's Architecture Vision, which will also help achieve the segment architecture.

D. TECHNOLOGY ARCHITECTURE PHASE

Next, those conducting the work at the Project Level will look deeper into the technology architecture supporting the applications, develop the starting point and the Target Architecture, and assess whether there are other risks or needs present prior to implementation on their assigned project. This means that the team member in charge of the employee data project may assess whether there could be any loss of data as a result of the planned infrastructure upgrades.

For example, if three of the nine business units are on one type of operating system, and the other six are on another, they may need to look at whether the infrastructure requires adjustments before they begin to synchronize the data. This will, by extension, also affect the MDM capabilities, as that project may not be able to proceed until the data consolidation project is completed. By identifying those gaps in the technology infrastructure, the enterprise can mitigate any risks or further narrow down the best plan toward optimization.

E. OPPORTUNITIES AND SOLUTIONS PHASE

Like the higher levels, this phase will consolidate all of the information gathered for the vision, business, data, applications, and technology phases but focuses upon the assigned project to create its initial roadmap. This will help define the transition architectures that are needed, further assess the readiness and risk of the transformation to take place, and finalize the project's Target Architecture.

Next, the project's implementation and migration strategy is developed, and defined Work Packages are established. At the Project Level, these are the specific steps that need to take place to accomplish the transformation, so for consolidating the data, it may look like this:

- Work Package 1: Migrate data from source 1 to transition architecture.

- Work Package 2: Migrate data from source 2 to transition architecture.

- Work Package 3: Migrate data from source 3 to transition architecture.

- Work Package 4: Transfer ownership of transition architecture to the team member in charge of data review.

- Work Package 5: Review data for redundancies or missing data.

- Work Package 6: Finalize data consolidation.

None of these Work Packages are completed quite yet but are being "mapped out" to ensure consistency across the process and alignment with the established vision.

For the MDM project, the Work Packages may look something like the following:

- Work Package 1: Research the various available data management solutions, including their pros and cons and associated costs.

- Work Package 2: Create an implementation plan based upon risk assessment findings and the technology infrastructure.

- Work Package 3: Analyze solutions and create a comprehensive report of findings to present for governance approval.

- Work Package 4: Perform transition architecture for data migration to mitigate any business disruption.

- Work Package 5: Deploy new MDM solution.

F. MIGRATION PLANNING PHASE

Here, this phase will finalize the Architecture Roadmap for the assigned project along with the project's implementation and migration plan, including any additional cost analysis that needs to be considered. Like at the higher levels, there will be documentation completed about what has been learned that could help inform best practices for other projects or the next cycle of EA.

G. IMPLEMENTATION GOVERNANCE PHASE

At the Capability Level, there may not be much governance performed other than confirming that the project is aligned with the strategic vision and that approval has been granted for the work.

H. ARCHITECTURE CHANGE MANAGEMENT PHASE

In this final phase, the roadmap for the assigned project has been completed and will outline the specific actions that need to be taken for implementation and transformation. As with the higher levels, it will also consider the maintenance of the architecture life cycle, confirm that the governance framework is being executed in alignment with the overall vision and goals, and validate that the project changes will meet the required capabilities. There may be additional monitoring tools or practices defined at the Project Level that sync up with those at the Segment Level for additional risk management and for facilitating feedback on the implementation of the project.

As you can see, this is a lot of work and a mountain of information to maintain, as the ADM is tailored for each level of architecture. As Enterprise Architects, we find that our entire goal is to help shepherd enterprises through this process because we know it can quickly feel overwhelming. But the past has taught us that this systematic approach of checks and balances is the most thorough way to ensure stability throughout the EA process and mitigate risk, ultimately saving the enterprise time and money on the path to growth and Agility.

Conclusion

To leave you with one more analogy of these concepts, let's go back for a second to college days. You could think of the Strategic Level as your major, your desired end goal for your degree. The Segment Level could be viewed as the credit requirements and necessary classes that your advisor helps you figure out that will lead to that degree. Finally, the Capability/Project Level could be seen as the classes themselves, with the Work Packages being the assignments and exams completed in each class.

Meanwhile, the partitions could be seen as how you divide up your coursework and your schedule, how you prioritize the requirements, such as deciding whether you will take summer courses or whether you will get your basics out of the way first or gradually fit them in between your major studies. Partitioning could even include deciding whether you take classes each day or schedule a day off to catch up on writing reports, or choosing a specific professor over another.

While all of this requires a lot of thought, intention, and planning, I don't think anyone would argue against the idea that this helps bring clarity to the process of a college education. Likewise, by understanding the levels of architecture and how they interact and impact one another, it brings clarity and intention to the EA process.

Enterprise transformation is complicated, but partitioning the architecture and understanding the levels helps divide up the responsibility so that no one single person or team is overwhelmed with accomplishing the transformation on top of their day-to-day responsibilities. While the timeline and drivers will be determined at the Enterprise Level, the Segment- and Capability-Level teams ensure that the work is carried out strategically and efficiently.

After all, plans are only good if they are followed up by actions, but knowing the three levels helps with both putting together plans *and* actions. With that being said, the key to everything discussed thus far is the actual implementation of new capabilities and the development of the architecture to optimize the business from the top down.

CHAPTER TAKEAWAYS

▶ Trying to deal with all architecture aspects at once is too cumbersome, so partitioning is essential to make the process manageable.

▶ Selecting the right partition of architecture combined with the right level makes the architecture more flexible and easier to integrate.

▶ The Strategic Level is focused on enterprise-wide goals, determined by the drivers influencing the change.

▶ The Segment Level is focused on the program or portfolio areas that need to be addressed to help achieve the Strategic-Level initiatives.

▶ The Capability Level is focused on Project-Level tasks and actions that need to be taken to achieve the Segment-Level initiatives in order to accomplish the Strategic-Level transformation.

▶ The nine phases of the ADM are tailored at each level as a consistent and thorough approach to ensure alignment with the goals of the enterprise and consideration of all four architecture domains.

CHAPTER 8

PHASES OF BUSINESS CAPABILITY DEVELOPMENT

Imagine for a moment that you decide to go fishing, but you have never fished before. You walk into your local sporting goods store and head over to the fishing supplies. It's packed full of many options for all the necessities: different types of rods, reels, a large variety of colored lures, hooks, and even tackle boxes for storing all these items.

Now imagine that a store employee—one with experience in fishing—walks up and asks, "May I help you?" As you are someone who has never gone fishing, it would make sense to accept the offer, but let us pretend that you say, "No, I don't need any help." You spend an hour or two walking up and down the aisles, making selections, and then second-guessing those selections without any insight or input into what rod might be best for a novice fisher or what lures would be best for different fish. Besides wasting time, you might also walk out buying more supplies than necessary or buying the wrong supplies altogether.

But let's say that you decide to accept help from the employee. They ask you, "What are you looking for?"

"I've never gone fishing, but I'd like to try it out."

"Great," they answer. "What kind of fish are you hoping to catch?"

You haven't even thought about that yet, so then the employee tells you about a couple of nearby fishing holes that other customers have recommended, including what kind of fish are in those lakes. From there, the employee is able to start recommending some specific lures and a good rod and reel for you.

You spend twenty or thirty minutes in the store, buying only the essentials because you had input from someone who understands fishing better than you, and then you head out to enjoy a new hobby and hopefully a few catches to celebrate.

In many ways, this is exactly the role of the Enterprise Architect in the EA process—to provide the expertise and broad knowledge of the frameworks and tailor them to fit the organization's needs in the same way the sporting goods employee will tailor recommendations to the customer's needs. Likewise, Enterprise Architects provide domain expertise, meaning that we can provide a level of collective knowledge for the client's industry. They may be the experts in terms of the condition of their specific business and what needs to be changed, but we bring considerable value in helping them identify the most essential transformations by looking at the latest trends in their industries and the aspects they may be missing that their competitors are already implementing.

> This is exactly the role of the Enterprise Architect in the EA process—to provide the expertise and broad knowledge of the frameworks and tailor them to fit the organization's needs.

Up to this point, much of our discussion has focused on high-level concepts and understanding the nature and necessity of Enterprise Architecture. But here, we will talk more about the actual performance of the architecture, or what we Enterprise Architects refer to as the business capability development.

While I hope you have seen throughout this book the role that the Enterprise Architect plays and the value we provide in consulting and guiding the process, from framework selection to establishing governance, I want to show more specifically the role we play in helping the enterprise transform step by step. As I already mentioned, the process and industry expertise is where we can help streamline things to make the process the most effective and efficient. In a sense, you could say we optimize the process for the organization's optimization.

But we also assist in bringing all of the stakeholders onto the same page. After all, many organizations are fully capable of discovering areas of improvement on their own, but having an external perspective can help them identify their blind spots. It is easier to create some unison and synchronicity between the stakeholders when a neutral party enters the picture to help align things. Often when we are hired by an organization, this external perspective ends up being one of the greatest advantages, as we assist them in finding the problems and corresponding solutions they did not even know to look for.

Think about it this way: members of an enterprise tend to think mostly about their specific area of specialization. The C-Suite may be most concerned with the shareholders and market developments, developers are thinking only about development, the sales team is focused on sales, operations people are busy with operations, and so on. Enterprise architects are able to zoom out to have a broad perspective of the whole enterprise, but they can also zoom in to understand how each discipline within the enterprise operates.

So while we may not be the ones "catching the fish"—that is, doing the actual work within the company—we ensure that the organization is in optimal shape for getting that work done.

Regardless of the organization or industry, establishing the business capability involves three phases:

- Planning

- Implementation

- Operation

Now let's take a look at each one of these individually to see how they work within the EA process.

Phase 1: Planning/Architecture Development

This first phase encompasses everything we have discussed in the book thus far, so obviously I won't rehash everything here. Suffice it to say that the Planning Phase is the core of Enterprise Architecture, laying a strong foundation for any transformation.

The key components of this Planning Phase (as we saw in chapter 4) are as follows:

- Process

- Content

- Reusable building blocks

As Enterprise Architects, we will help the enterprise with all the components of this Development Phase, including the following:

- Selecting the frameworks to utilize

- Tailoring the framework for the enterprise, including tailoring with any industry-specific reference architectures

- Identifying the content to address the four domains of business, data, applications, and technology

- Establishing the repositories for maintaining all of the information gathered

It's worth mentioning that the assistance we provide with the frameworks is of particular value, as these can be difficult to understand in both their application and execution. This is one of the reasons that Enterprise Architects have to go through a rigorous certification process before they can utilize TOGAF® with clients. Just like you wouldn't want an unapproved architect designing your building, the same can be said for your Enterprise Architecture.

Phase 2: Implementation

During this phase, where new technology or processes are being implemented, the Enterprise Architect assists by establishing touch points between the various disciplines within the organization to ensure smooth implementation from end to end.

This is especially true in more complex organizations. With Southeast Regional Bank, it was not only the business units that had to be considered, but the various disciplines within them, as each unit had its own HR department, sales department, operations team, and so on. Therefore, it was our role to coordinate the disciplines within each business unit but also between the business units to catch any gaps in the implementation process before they became bigger problems that might slow down or derail the EA process.

To better understand what a smooth Implementation Phase looks like, we typically break it down into five parts:

- Design

- Build

- Test

- Package

- Deploy

DESIGN

The design portion of implementation refers to the low-level design, or rather, the design of each component needed so that code can be generated to accomplish the necessary work. From a strategic view, you begin with the high-level design—the end goal or vision to be accomplished—then break it down into smaller components, doing the more detailed design.

With Southeast Regional Bank, one of their needs was to implement a standard CRM shared across all business units. Therefore, that need becomes an input for the Implementation Phase, which means that the CRM itself needs to be designed. While designing the CRM, you then go into more details, such as the components that it needs to contain, the data inputs, the interfaces for it to function, and the specific services it needs to interact with.

Now let's say a company already has an existing solution for the need. In the case of CRM, let's say that the company is already using their own system they have created. Rather than simply check off the box and say, "We've already done this," the enterprise needs to take a step back and perform the due diligence to see if the active solution still fits the needs of the enterprise and whether it is aligned with the strategic vision that has been set. If not, then the enterprise must be willing to step away from that solution and take the necessary steps to find a new one.

But if a company is starting from a blank slate where no solution is in place, there can be a temptation to choose the latest software solution instead of taking the time to consider what design the solution should take for the specific architecture being developed. This is because if you rush into the decision and discover later it was the wrong solution, and you have to find a new one, then you have wasted time and resources.

Unfortunately, this second scenario is one of the greatest pitfalls I see made with organizations. They select a solution without understanding their requirements or architecture; then halfway through the implementation process, they realize it's not the right solution. And then sometimes, when they go back to management to request moving to a new solution, they struggle to get the approval because the budget was already used, or else they are too afraid to go to management with the request and deploy a new solution without permission, which can create confusion, at the very least.

Another practical example is when a company is restructuring and decides they are going to move half of their workforce to remote work permanently. This decision to move half of their workforce to remote work is on the Strategic Level of the Enterprise Architecture, which then prompts the design portion. In other words, you're not selecting a solution yet (e.g., Zoom, Microsoft Teams, etc.) but rather asking the questions about what design will support the remote staff:

- How many of our staff will be working from home?

- What are their specific needs for their role(s)?

- Do they need traditional phone call capabilities or only video chat? Do they need both?

The answers to these analytical questions will dictate the design of the solution that will then be built, whether it is being built internally or built by a third party.

BUILD

The second part of implementation involves taking the design that was established and then selecting a solution that meets those needs, whether by building the solution or purchasing it from the market.

There may be situations in which an enterprise literally builds their own solution for the design that was established, prompted by the specific needs of the enterprise, their capability to build their own solution, or because no other solution is available in the market. There may also be situations, especially when it comes to technology solutions, where the enterprise will select a solution that has already been built and exists within the marketplace for purchase and implementation.

So, returning to the previous example of a company moving half of their staff to work remotely, the company will take the information gathered during the design portion and decide to select Microsoft Teams as their solution. But beyond simply choosing the solution, the build portion also involves the work that must be done to make it available for the staff. This includes purchasing the licenses and installing the software on all the necessary devices across the company to ensure that everyone has the ability to use it.

TEST

Now, whether the code is built or purchased by the enterprise, it needs to be tested to see whether it satisfies the specific need of the design. The chosen solution will be tested to confirm that everything is working properly, which may involve creating some scenarios or test cases and then analyzing whether it truly works or not. This could include load testing a selected software or any other action that might be taken to identify any possible defects that may need to be addressed.

With our remote work example, this might look like the enterprise testing Microsoft Teams by using it on multiple types of devices and on different networks, making test calls between remote workers and those still in an office setting, and even running some mock meetings to ensure it is working the way it should—and if not, identifying why not. Testing is not carried out enterprise-wide but among a chosen group usually determined by the EA Team.

An Enterprise Architect plays an important role during the testing portion by helping establish some quality gates the enterprise will utilize to determine whether the solution is performing up to optimal standards. Now let us say that things are not working the way they should—perhaps there are a lot of bugs, a lot of issues that are system errors—the Enterprise Architect will be reviewing these throughout the implementation project at each stage.

Ideally, the Enterprise Architect will help identify potential issues before the Testing Phase occurs and address these in the design or build portion. But there are times where testing shows that the design needs to be modified, and the Enterprise Architect will guide the organization in fixing the issues that have been revealed, whether the issues are being caused by the application itself or from some issue with the technology infrastructure itself.

It's essential, though, for the Enterprise Architect to be receiving feedback at each interval or quality gate to catch these issues and resolve them as they arise so that the implementation process can move forward without creating more problems and meet all of the needs that were established during the design.

It's also key during testing for the regulatory governance to be involved to provide the oversight of whether the actions taken are being done according to the strategic plan that was developed in the beginning. A software solution may test perfectly, but if it is not aligned with the strategy and vision, then it is ultimately not going to help the enterprise optimize in the long run.

> An Enterprise Architect plays an important role during the testing portion by helping establish some quality gates the enterprise will utilize to determine whether the solution is performing up to optimal standards.

PACKAGE

Packaging is simply the part of the process that must occur before the solution can be effectively deployed. Once the code is ready, then it must be stored in a configuration management tool before deployment. Without being too technical, though, the overall purpose in packaging is to streamline and standardize the way in which a larger organization can deliver the software solution to the devices for all the end users. Often, there is an application package for each software solution that is being implemented.

For example, many solutions already have a packaging method specific to them: Java has one, a CRM solution may have its own, the payroll software will have its own, and so on. Regardless of whether it has its own packaging or whether the enterprise has to develop one, there must be a plan in place for how the software will be packaged and ultimately deployed.

The Enterprise Architect will also help guide this process to ensure that the packaging is optimal for deployment, to catch any possible issues that could derail deployment, and to help finalize the timing for each piece of software to be deployed into operation. Overlooking the packaging process could slow down deployment, leading to delays or additional costs.

DEPLOY

Finally, implementation is completed with deploying the solution across the enterprise from the configuration management tool. Once the solution has been packaged, the operations team is responsible for getting it into wider use. Nowadays, it's not unusual for the deployment to happen through a cloud environment, though other methods could be used, depending on the solution.

Once the delivery is made, then the solution will be available to the end users. Typically, there is a UAT (User Acceptance Test) utilized so the enterprise can validate the adoption rate of the solution among the end users. Often, software vendors will offer a three-month warranty period following the deployment so that any issues that arise can be addressed.

While I've focused here on implementation more than technology solutions, it's important to understand that this methodology can also apply to business processes. For example, an enterprise looking to establish a new mission statement could also go through these same steps:

- Design: What needs to be included in the mission statement? What do we want it to communicate? What will be its purpose? How do we want it to drive decision making?

- Build: What is the best wording that will express our mission to both staff and customers?

- Testing: What do others think about the selected wording? Is it clear? Is there anything that needs to be tweaked?

- Packaging: How will the new mission statement be announced to the organization? How will it be presented to the public?

- Deploying: This occurs when the new mission statement is officially revealed and implemented across the enterprise.

Following this methodology under the guidance of a knowledgeable Enterprise Architect will help in fostering an environment in which the right solutions—technology or otherwise—can be thoughtfully selected and implemented with minimal risk for the organization.

Phase 3: Operations

When an enterprise reaches the Operations Phase, this is where you see the application of SLAs (service level agreements) and OLAs (operational level agreements). As Enterprise Architects, we find our first responsibility is to help establish the content of these agreements and ensure that the operations team is meeting the terms of the agreements.

Another responsibility we have during this phase is resolving any incidents that may arise. At any time new technology has been implemented, there will be issues that come up, so we are usually collecting vast amounts of information during the Operations Phase to identify, isolate, and resolve those issues as they arise.

During operations, data is continuously being collected from the implementation of the new software or process. Systems and operations will be monitored by the Enterprise Systems (ES) and metrics collected, such as whether the systems being deployed are meeting the established SLAs or OLAs. If these agreements and specifications are not being met, then that information will go into the input for the next iteration for rearchitecting.

Therefore, any information gathered in the Operations Phase can be input back into the Strategy Phase so that when the enterprise is conducting their next EA cycle, it can be put to use for developing a new strategy. While it is the role of the operations team to collect that data, it's the role of the Enterprise Architect to present the information to the Architecture Board to interpret the data at an Enterprise Level so that no inputs are missed that could help the organization succeed.

ITIL Frameworks

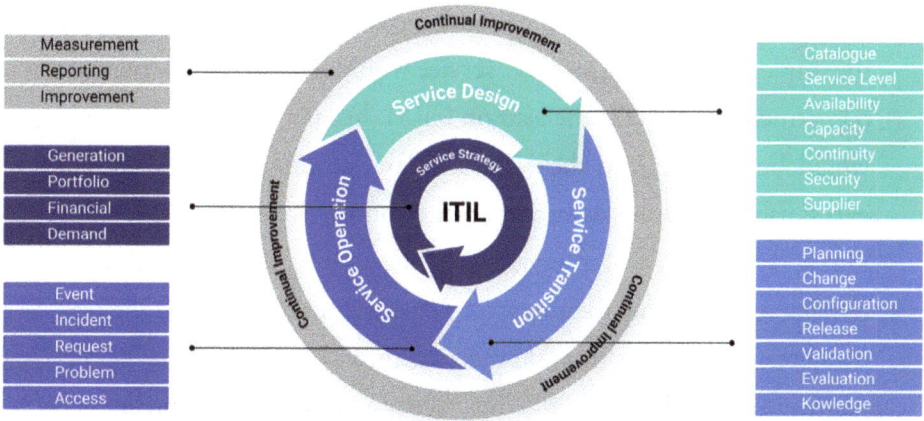

When guiding an organization through this phase of implementation, it is encouraged for the operations team to use a standard framework, such as the Information Technology Infrastructure Library (ITIL) framework. While this framework is not part of the ADM within TOGAF® or any of the other frameworks we have already discussed, it is a tool to help manage the various information being collected so that it can be properly analyzed and understood, as the enterprise seeks continual improvement with each iteration of the EA process.

Besides being a simple organizational model, the ITIL provides the operations team with the opportunity to notice any new issues that may have arisen since the Implementation Phase, problems that need to be managed, and other considerations for optimizing the enterprise. The Enterprise Architects can then provide the additional insight and expertise to process the data.

For example, let's go back to the roadmap that we established for Southeast Regional Bank. They needed to develop a single MDM and a single CRM; they needed new tools for finance accounting, a new integration platform, and new HR systems; and they needed for digitization to be done. Not all of the same teams would be performing the implementation—customer service would handle MDM, the sales department would take the lead on CRM, human resources obviously would be looking into the HR tools, and so on—but they are not necessarily consulting with one another on the tools they are looking into and how they will integrate with one another. Instead, each team is going off and doing their own implementation aligned with the plan they created, whether they are meeting their standards and principles that were established, and whether they are meeting their timelines.

Operations will be monitoring all of these moving parts via the ITIL framework, but the Enterprise Architects will assume the governance role by supervising the various implementations and corresponding data to ensure that all is going according to plan. From a bottom-line perspective, it is during this phase in which the services offered will be consumed by anyone among the end users. This is the service offer that can help provide insight into how often the solution is being utilized and what the cost of its utilization is in contrast to its value, and it can create the hard data that can prove the implementation was a success from the perspective of Return on Investment (ROI).

Conclusion

It's essential to note here that implementation is not a one-and-done event within the EA process. There will be multiple phases of implementation for multiple capabilities throughout the various stages of TOGAF®'s ADM. After all, you can imagine the nightmare it would be if an enterprise attempted to implement all of their new tools, software, and processes all at once. It would make the data collection of what is working and what issues need resolving more complicated. Rather, implementation takes place in strategic and planned steps to make it more manageable for everyone—from the Architecture Board, to the Enterprise Architect, to the stakeholders.

The same can be said of the other phases of business capability development. As we will discuss in the final chapter, in which we will cover the concept of Agility, the EA process is one that helps organizations optimize and innovate over the long term, not a one-time project like a box to check off the task list.

To go back to our fishing example, you can think of it the same way. Someone taking up the hobby of fishing doesn't spend the time, effort, and investment in getting the proper gear if they are only planning to go fishing one time or if they only want to catch one fish. Rather, they want the best gear available to catch as many fish as they can for as long as they can. Over time, they will revisit the sporting goods store to seek out a better rod, new lures, or a new tackle box for their growing collection of gear.

Whether they are using the right equipment could be quantified in the number of fish they catch, though they will also need to take into consideration environmental factors: Is the lake I'm using being overfished by others? Is it time to invest in a boat? Do I have adequate storage space for catching the number of fish I know I'm capable of?

Translating this into business terms, enterprises must ask similar questions: Has the marketplace changed? Where can we find new customers? How can we streamline processes to generate more revenue? Do we have the physical and technological infrastructure in place to serve more customers, or will we inadvertently turn them away because we cannot accommodate the demand?

Finding the right answers for these questions is the very reason that I founded SNA Technologies. As Enterprise Architects, we want the same thing that every enterprise wants: to see them succeed in their endeavors and develop new ways to succeed. Even the greatest athletes need coaches on the road to success; therefore we can help coach enterprises to build the most successful architecture possible.

CHAPTER TAKEAWAYS

▶ An important advantage of hiring an Enterprise Architect is that they can have the broad understanding and external perspective of the whole enterprise, which can sometimes be lost by those within the enterprise.

▶ The first phase of business capability development is planning/architecture development in which the strategy is set. Developing a clear strategy and vision is essential for optimal implementation; otherwise, it is like constructing a building without a blueprint.

▶ The second phase is implementation, which can be broken up into five stages: design, build, test, package, and deploy. If the Enterprise Architecture is already done in the first phase, then the correct solutions/requirements will be selected.

▶ The third phase is operations, in which information is continuously collected to ensure optimization is occurring and agreements are being met, and it is used to create inputs for the next iteration of EA optimization. A major pitfall for organizations is believing the process is complete with implementation and having no follow-up occurring through operational feedback.

▶ During the Operations Phase, Enterprise Architects are responsible for providing governance, aligning the information being collected with the strategy, fixing any problem areas as they arise, and identifying key areas for improvement during the next round of optimization.

CHAPTER 9

AGILITY IN THREE PHASES

When you hear the word "Agility," what first comes to mind? For many, the mind turns to the world of athletics—perhaps the image of two fencers and the clash of their rapiers as they parry with one another, or a tennis pro moving deftly with an outstretched arm to swat a match-winning stroke, or else a basketball star outmaneuvering the opposing team's defense to make a layup.

Certainly, the versatility and speed of such athletes is part of the attraction of sports, and I think this gives us a good, but incomplete, picture of Agility as it pertains to business. I say "incomplete" because where, in sports, Agility is a means to an end—that is, it helps the athlete win a contest—Agility in business is a means but *not* an end.

With improvement comes the opportunity to face new challenges, and the Agile business is one that is more versatile to meet the challenges of the changing marketplace, able to incorporate the best tools to achieve the best possible results. As I alluded to at the end of the previous chapter, we can again find a parallel between the worlds of sports and business, as very few—if any—

> Agility in business is a means but *not* an end.

athletes reach the highest ranks of their discipline without the help of a knowledgeable coach to guide them in the right practices and tools to succeed. Likewise, this is the role of the Enterprise Architect, to "coach" the enterprise in the right practices and tools to achieve business Agility.

Everything we've discussed thus far has been leading up to this point: understanding how an Enterprise Architect and the EA process can help an organization optimize through Agility. Achieving true end-to-end Agility for an enterprise requires incorporating Agile practices in each phase: planning, implementation, and operations.

With Southeast Regional Bank, we wanted to not only help them streamline the enterprise through updated technology and processes but also to guide them into an Agile culture. This meant there had to be an ownership and desire for Agility, not only among their C-Suite but at every level of the organization, so that they could continue to improve over the long term.

Defining Agility

To begin with, I like to define Agility based on its intent. At its heart, Agility is about working smarter, not harder—and where Agility is enabled by technology solutions but is driven by management so that it becomes a part of the culture. The Agile enterprise is one whose architecture is able to pivot with marketplace transformations, driven by a customer-centric vision, and remain competitive through innovation. It is not the destination itself but rather the engine that moves the enterprise toward its destination.

Striving for Agility without a clear sense of vision is like driving in a new place without a map. You might see some nice sights along the way, but you will waste a lot of time and fuel doing so, or you might accidentally end up on the dangerous side of town. Agility has to start with one simple question: "What do you want to accomplish?"

One of the great pitfalls I see with enterprises pursuing Agility is that they may know what they want to accomplish, but they spend too much time planning and not enough time taking action and solving problems. True business Agility means taking action, like an athlete. An athlete or team may have the goal to win their match and even spend hours talking about strategy and plays, but at the end of the day, that will mean nothing if they do not act upon it.

Establishing an Agile methodology alongside the EA process fosters an environment in which optimization and innovation can be happening continuously. After all, business Agility is not a single project or initiative for an enterprise to cross off its checklist but should persist as a collective mindset throughout the organization.

As I see it, Agility happens in three phases:

Strategy/Planning—>Implementation—>Operations

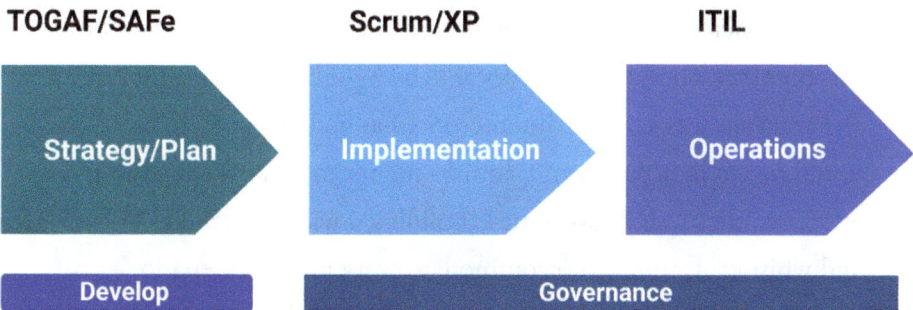

TOGAF/SAFe	Scrum/XP	ITIL
Strategy/Plan	Implementation	Operations
Develop	Governance	

It is no accident that these phases are exactly the same as the ones we discussed in the last chapter. While Agility should be occurring in each of these phases, the highest level of Agile transformation tends to take place during the Implementation Phase since this is typically where the new technology solutions or business processes are being put into play.

A bad practice that I've seen by some organizations is pushing their Planning Phase into their Implementation Phase instead of keeping it separate. This is often for the same reason I mentioned above: they spend too much time planning instead of taking action to the point that when they are on the verge of implementation, they backtrack and do more planning than what is necessary, afraid of doing the wrong thing so much that they end up doing nothing.

> Business Agility is not a single project or initiative for an enterprise to cross off its checklist but should persist as a collective mindset throughout the organization.

But by starting with a clear vision and aligning their plan to that vision, an enterprise can build confidence that they are taking the right actions and efficiently pursue Agility and optimization. While many organizations can understand and agree with Agility on this higher, more philosophical level, where they often run into problems is in the practical application of Agility.

Another pitfall I have seen with some organizations is adopting practices that, on the surface, appear to be Agile but work against Agility. For example, let's say that the enterprise has built a new CRM software to roll out to their sales team. In the attempt to make it something for everyone, they spend lots of time building a wide assortment of "bells and whistles" features to accommodate every possible scenario.

This seems "Agile" because they think they are making the solution helpful by adding in so many features, but what this actually does is make it more difficult for the end users/stakeholders (i.e., the sales team) to learn and implement the software. In this scenario, not only has the development team wasted time and resources adding in a lot of features that were ultimately unnecessary, but it actually creates more work for the end users rather than streamlining the process.

Instead, it may be better—and more Agile—to start off simple with the end user in mind and, if additional features need to be added later on, making those changes with a Baseline First approach.

Another misconception about Agile is that the focus has to be all on the details, and therefore, the greatest energy must be spent on planning. This leads to a scenario in which the enterprise is always talking, always planning to *do* Agile, rather than taking action to *be* Agile. If there is no action being taken, then it is not truly an Agile practice, no matter how detailed and thorough the plan. When an enterprise becomes too tactical in their pursuit of Agility, time and resources are being wasted instead of solving problems.

True Agile practices, however, keep the end user/stakeholder front and center, asking for continuous feedback so that waste can be eliminated from the process and to ensure that their problems are being solved and needs are being met. Therefore, some core attributes of Agility could be defined as the following:

- Flexibility: Can the solutions selected be adapted for changing needs and encourage innovation?

- Cost: Do the solutions make the enterprise more cost effective? What is the ROI?

- Speed of Response: How quickly are the solutions being developed and implemented?

- Quality: Does the solution increase the quality of products/ services by eliminating waste and increasing value for customers?

- Reusability: Can the solutions be reused across the enterprise to help enable multiple drivers or fulfill multiple capability requirements?

It's important to note here that this is not a simple checklist but that these attributes often inform one another. Some might balk at the attribute of Speed of Response and say, "But I thought we needed to be intentional with selecting a solution, not just pick the quickest one?" And that's true—you should spend time to make sure the solution is aligned with the overall strategic vision. Nor do you have to be perfect the first time, as being Agile technically means you can iterate as often as needed. However, you have to balance the number of times you iterate with cost. If you iterate too many times, then you are not being quick *or* cost effective.

You could see a similar scenario with the attributes of cost and reusability. For example, with Southeast Regional Bank, there was a lack of communication between their business units regarding CMS, which was one of their drivers. They had multiple solutions/applications being used, so this situation featured neither flexibility or quality, or aided speed of response—not to mention cost. By selecting a single reusable solution, they were able to address all of those attributes to become a more Agile enterprise.

But having a clear definition of Agile is not enough. What does it actually look like within the three phases of strategy, implementation, and operations? How do the three phases impact one another and encourage Agility rather than stifle it?

TOPAGILE METHODOLOGY

As SNA Technologies has worked on the forefront of the EA industry and helped organizations for fifteen years, I've had the opportunity to create a methodology for developing Agility called TopAgile. We used this methodology with Southeast Regional Bank and continue to use it with our clients, so you could view it as a sort of "sneak peek" for how we would help your enterprise achieve Agility.

Because it is designed to work alongside TOGAF®, it can readily be adapted for any organization in any industry so that the Enterprise Architecture can be done in a more Agile manner. But even if an enterprise is using another framework, like Zachman, the same methodology can be used to the same effect.

At its most basic, TopAgile is conducted along the three levels of architecture (Strategic, Segment, and Capability) that we discussed in chapter 7. At each of these levels, there will be four iteration cycles, which create a natural flow of high-level to low-level Agility from end to end.

Agile Enterprise Architecture Methodology

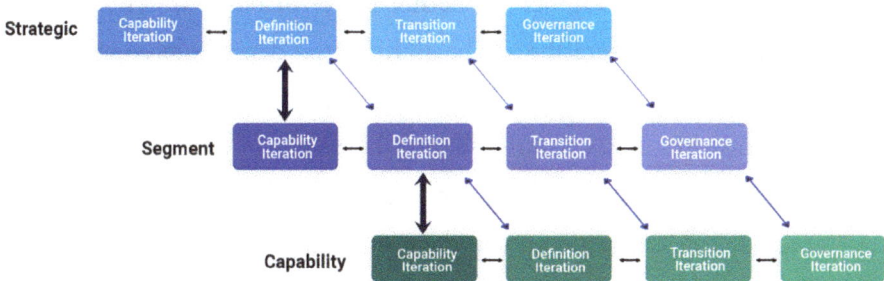

Strategic	Capability Iteration	Definition Iteration	Transition Iteration	Governance Iteration		
Segment		Capability Iteration	Definition Iteration	Transition Iteration	Governance Iteration	
Capability			Capability Iteration	Definition Iteration	Transition Iteration	Governance Iteration

Remember, the Strategic Level (number 1) is the Enterprise-Level architecture where the long-term vision is established. In the first block (1.1), Capability Iteration, this is where the enterprise asks itself, "Where do we need to be over the next ten to thirty years?" staying at the high-level view without getting into specific details. From there, it will then be broken down into increments of a two-to-five-year vision, partitioning the timeline into more manageable pieces.

From there, the enterprise moves to the second block (1.2), Definition Iteration. Because we are still in the Strategic Level, though, this is where the enterprise will develop a high-level strategy for both their business model and their technology model. Instead of getting into the "nitty gritty" details of business or technology, you're looking at the "bare minimum" of what you need at that level, what we would call the MVA (Minimum Viable Architecture). When that MVA is identified, you move on to the next level, and so on, cascading down each level. At the Strategic Level, you are simply identifying the partitions and identifying their dependencies, which will give context to the next level down, the Segment Level.

So once those are defined, you can follow the arrow down to the Segment Level (2) and do a quick check on the Architecture Capabilities (2.1) that are required for each partition. From there, you move to the Definition Iteration (2.2) of the Segment Level to define the approach for each segment, whether target or baseline. This means you develop one iteration of the architecture definitions so that you can have a clear set of capabilities outlined.

Now this allows you to get into the details of the required capabilities for each segment, so you follow the line down to the Capability Level (3). Here again, you will do a quick check on the Architecture Capabilities (3.1) to ensure they are aligned with the requirements defined in the Segment Level. Just like before, you will then define one iteration of the capabilities that will fulfill the need that was established in the Segment Level.

From there, we will remain at the Capability Level and head into the Transition Iteration block (3.3), where implementation will occur, which then feeds into the Governance Iteration (3.4). As we discussed in the last chapter, this governance aspect will provide the checks and balances to make sure that the capabilities are meeting the requirements set at the Segment Level but also the vision that was set at the Strategic Level. Therefore, as implementation is occurring, you are making sure that the capabilities are compliant with the strategic, segment, and capability architectures.

In other words, you don't have to figure out everything all at once. You can start with the "big picture" and break it down into smaller chunks along the way. One advantage to this is a simplification of the process so that it is not so daunting, but it also allows you to be more detail oriented and get to work quicker.

So to bring this into context, let's return to Southeast Regional Bank, applying the TopAgile Model. At the Strategic Level, the high-level vision would be defined as:

"Over the next ten to thirty years, Southeast Regional Bank will develop into a one-stop shop for financial services."

That is then broken down into smaller chunks:

"In the next two to five years, we will be able to cross-sell products to customers across our business units."

In order to define the partitions, though, you have to not only have an established vision, but you also have to spend time brainstorming the drivers and their corresponding enablers. For example:

DRIVER		ENABLER
Establish Single View of Customer	⟷	MDM (Master Data Management)
Cross-Sell Products	⟷	CRM (Customer Relations Management)
Improve Financial Reporting	⟷	Accounting Software, Standardized Practice
Consolidate Physical Assets	⟷	Close ⅓ of Locations

These drivers and enablers make up the Strategic Level's Definition Iteration for Southeast Regional Bank. Now obviously, they could not do all of these things at once, so before plunging into these segments, we worked with them to put together a roadmap and timeline for each segment. The Architecture Board looked back at their established vision of becoming a one-stop shop for financial services and decided which of these segments needed to take priority and how quickly they wanted it done.

So for the sake of simplicity, we will say that they chose "Establish Single View of Customer" as their first segment to tackle. In order to enable that single view, they knew they needed an MDM that is shared across all of the business units. In their case, each business unit was using its own management tool, its own process, so these needed to be synced up. But before that could be done, the capabilities had to be defined. For each segment, there may be three or four capabilities that are defined and then a set of initiatives that make up those capabilities:

MDM CAPABILITIES	MDM INITIATIVES
Define the Baseline Business Unit Data Systems	What data is being collected?
	How is the data being stored?
	How is the data being updated?
Develop Target Enterprise Data Solutions	Collect and consolidate information from business units
	Research MDM software options
	Develop new enterprise MDM process
Implementation & Governance	Risk Assessment of selected MDM software
	Approval of selected MDM software
	Approval of new MDM process
	Implementation Plan

Depending on the order dictated by the roadmap and timeline that was established by the Architecture Board, you would then move on to the next driver-based objective. Perhaps with their new MDM established, Southeast Regional Bank would move on to CRM and begin the process of cross-selling for revenue generation, even as they looked into the other drivers, such as improved financial reporting or consolidating their physical assets.

With the TopAgile Methodology, there is a clear pattern of cascading and ascending with the decision-making and action processes so that each step remains aligned with the established vision. As each initiative is completed, the capabilities are met, satisfying each segment, which in turn satisfies the strategic architecture.

As we established early on, you can also see how this process sticks to what I consider the most important aspect of the EA process, which is keeping the business vision centered rather than centering the business around technology. Because the method can be adapted to any enterprise and repeated by any enterprise, it helps foster an environment in which Agile thinking becomes the norm in decision making at each level of the enterprise.

Also dependent upon the timeline and roadmap are changes that might need to be made along the way. Perhaps that is a change within the market that prompts a reordering of the business priorities. There also may be overlaps between the drivers and enablers. For example, building and implementing a new MDM at Southeast Regional Bank would also help enable aspects of cross-selling, selecting the appropriate CRM, and even improving the financial reporting. Your selected EA tools and repository help aid the enterprise in identifying those areas of overlap and addressing them strategically and with Agility.

To return to the sports analogy we began with, you can see how a coach influences an athlete to become more Agile through a disciplined approach. Perhaps they focus on certain drills on different days so that as new skills are learned, they become more natural for the athlete. They become a part of the "culture" for the athlete—or team—impacting their ability to remain competitive during competition.

Likewise, the Enterprise Architect serves as the coach in this methodology to help the enterprise learn the discipline of Agility. It will not occur on its own or without clear vision and intentionality, just as an athlete does not become a champion without clear vision and intentionality.

TOOLS FOR AGILITY

To become Agile across the three phases, there are a variety of tools that an Enterprise Architect may utilize alongside the methodology of each phase I've already described. In this way, you can approach each phase with some direction instead of starting from square one.

Strategy/Planning Phase

Because this phase is focused more on development, this is where you would utilize frameworks like TOGAF® and SAFe®. TOGAF®, of course, we have already spent a lot of time on, so let's talk a bit more about SAFe® (Scaled Agile Framework).

SAFe®, in version 5 as of 2020, is an Agile methodology that is composed of seven Core Competencies developed by Dean Leffingwell, and it works hand in hand with Lean techniques. These competencies consist of the following:

1. Lean-Agile Leadership

2. Team and Technical Agility

3. Agile Product Delivery

4. Enterprise Solution Delivery

5. Lean Portfolio Management

6. Organizational Agility

7. Continuous Learning Culture

These are not steps or phases in a process; rather, they serve to help an enterprise build a strong Agile foundation. They act as a kind of compass to ensure that the organization is headed in the right direction in terms of strategy. Additionally, the Enterprise Architect will help establish a small team that will be focused on implementing SAFe® Lean-Agile practices called the Lean-Agile Center of Excellence (LACE).

Keep in mind that SAFe® is no replacement for an EA framework like TOGAF® but is meant to work alongside it so that the Strategic- and Enterprise-Level decisions being made are keeping in line with Agile practices. This is done by measuring progress in business Agility along twenty-one dimensions through various assessment tools.

Implementation Phase

Since this phase falls into the area of governance, as does operations, it can utilize different methodologies to ensure Agility. Two such tools are Scrum and XP (Extreme Programming).

Scrum is a specific framework for utilizing an Agile perspective within product development and delivery and is a widely used method for project management. While it is not the simplest framework to utilize, this is yet another area where the Enterprise

> These are not steps or phases in a process; rather, they serve to help an enterprise build a strong Agile foundation. They act as a kind of compass to ensure that the organization is headed in the right direction in terms of strategy.

Architect can offer guidance and assistance.

SCRUM PROCESS

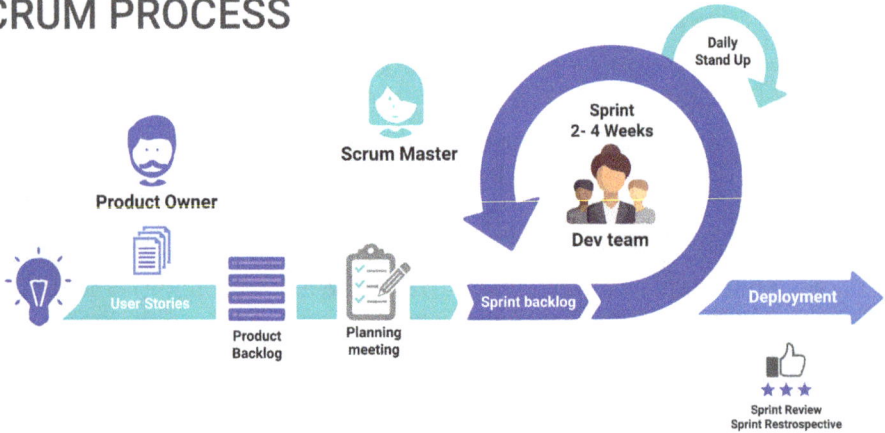

The main principles of Scrum to understand in our context can be summarized as follows:[6]

- Transparent information between all team members regarding the product or service being delivered

- Conducting regular inspections and evaluations so that adjustments can be made to the project when necessary

- Adapting the project with new measures based on the inspections and evaluations as needed

Furthermore, the Scrum life cycle is interspersed with meetings overseen by the Scrum Master to promote transparent sharing of information among all team members, including the user stories to maintain a customer-centric view, selecting key initiatives from the product backlog, and making necessary adjustments during the sprint

---

6   "Understanding Agile Scrum in 10 Minutes," https://www.tuleap.org/ (Tuleap, September 29, 2022), https://www.tuleap.org/agile/agile-scrum-in-10-minutes.

period when implementation is occurring prior to deployment. The sprint cycle is a period of two to four weeks when action is being taken based on the plan. As I mentioned before, a common problem for companies pursuing Agility is spending too much time planning, so following a Scrum cycle helps compel action and protect from overplanning without action. A truly Agile team will be able to communicate what actions are being taken during the sprint cycle, which will further protect from the temptation of being too tactical instead of actionable.

Another tool is Extreme Programming (XP), which is an iterative Agile methodology for software development with the intention to improve the quality of the software and improve the quality of life for the development team. Because of its specificity to software engineering, it won't be used in every EA situation, though its practices can be adapted and used within many contexts.

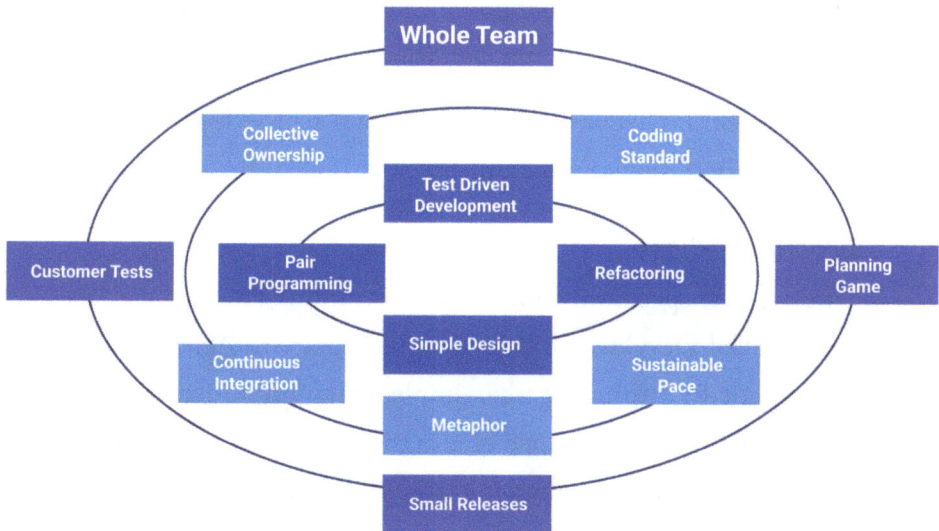

XP is based upon five values: communication, simplicity, feedback, courage, and respect. There are woven into its practices, as seen in the diagram on the previous page.

These practices utilize lots of feedback from both customers and team members as well as simplification and testing during the Implementation Phase. The name stems from its emphasis on encouraging teams to continuously test and practice code, almost to an "extreme" level in a continuous push for optimal implementation of the software.

XP emphasizes the role of programmers but also specifies other important roles throughout the process, such as the following:

- Testers: Individuals outside of the development team who help with testing the code

- Customers: End users who help make decisions about the product through customer stories

- Trackers: Individuals who use data to provide the team with feedback concerning the performance

- Coach: Individual who helps the team achieve higher performance throughout the process

Operations Phase

Before we talk specifically about the Operations Phase, there is a concept called DevOps, which is complementary to Agile software development by fusing together implementation and operations since both fall within the scope of governance. Simply put, DevOps combines an enterprise's cultural practices, philosophies, and tools to improve their ability to deliver their products at a high quality.

Now when it comes to operations itself, one tool to utilize within this phase is the ITIL framework, which stands for Information Technology Infrastructure Library. It lays a foundation for gauging the success of an initiative through best practices, especially in terms of delivering efficient support services.

ITIL Frameworks

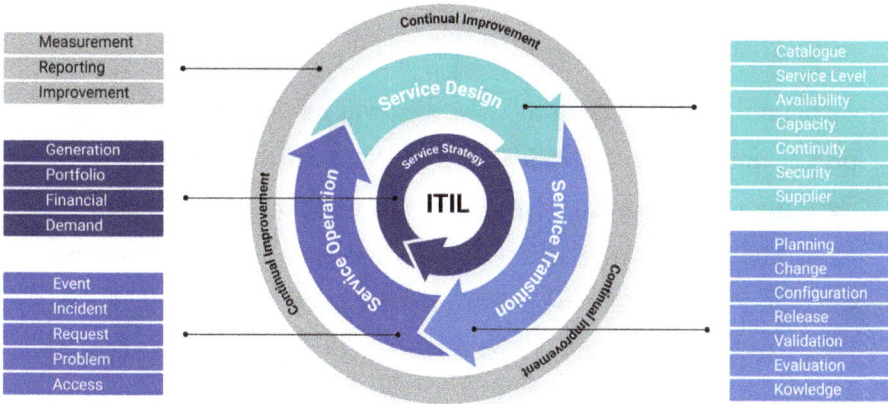

As seen in the diagram, there are three levels of the initiative life cycle, which is composed of five interdependent stages:

- Service Strategy (First Level)

- Service Design (Second Level)

- Service Transition (Second Level)

- Service Operation (Second Level)

- Continual Improvement (Third Level)

This framework operates well within the overall EA process because it keeps strategy centered while working toward ongoing progress and improvement. One must remember that within Agile, there is not an end point, but that being Agile means always working toward improvement in a way that will drive innovation and better serve the customer.

To return to the TopAgile Methodology, ITIL can be utilized with the Governance Iteration of each level, providing the continuous feedback required to ensure that the capabilities are not only being met but that they are also progressing.

FACTORS AFFECTING AGILITY

As helpful as all of these tools are, they will not succeed if the enterprise is not primed for Agility. Like our sports analogy, an athlete can have the greatest coach, the best equipment, and the best training plan, but if their mindset is wrong, then it is likely they will not succeed. Likewise, an enterprise's mindset must be in the right place before seeking to become Agile, and while in the process of pursuing Agility. In my own research and experience with guiding organizations through the EA process to become Agile, I've found a number of factors influencing their ability to do so.

Vision

As I mentioned already in the TopAgile Methodology, having a clear vision is key to success. An enterprise needs to establish this vision on three levels:

- First, there is the long-term vision, what they want to accomplish in the next ten to thirty years.

- Second, there is what I like to refer to as "near-term" vision, which is what they want to accomplish in the next two to five years.

- And then from there, the third level is broken down into smaller units of less than two years to define the short-term vision.

If an organization can have clear visions at all three of these levels—long term, near term, and short term—then it establishes a linkage between the levels that will foster operational efficiency.

Maturity

The next factor is the level of maturity of the enterprise. Earlier, we discussed the concept of sprints within the Scrum process, deploying smaller chunks of functionality at a fast rate within the Implementation Phase. Initiatives are a sprint, but enterprises have much longer life spans than initiatives, so they could be seen as a marathon.

But in many ways, becoming Agile is more like a marathon made up of sprints, like a type of relay race. And just as a new runner cannot go complete a marathon without first building up the abilities needed for the marathon, so it is with enterprises. They have to first make sure they are in a mature enough state of preparedness before becoming Agile.

To assess their maturity, an enterprise can utilize the Architecture Capability Maturity Model, which also fits into TOGAF®'s Architecture Development Method (ADM) during the Preliminary Phase. There are six possible maturity levels, which are ranked from 0 (least mature) to 5 (most mature) as follows:

- 0: None

- 1: Initial

- 2: Under Development

- 3: Defined

- 4: Managed

- 5: Measured

For a very large organization, I recommend that they have a level of at least a level 3 of maturity before pursuing Agility. If their assessment shows they are under a 3, then there are other improvements and transformations that need to take place within the enterprise before they should think about becoming Agile, simply because they are not yet in a state—or mindset—where it will successfully become a part of their culture. Instead, forcing Agility in this state could only make things more chaotic.

For a small to medium-sized organization, a level of 2—Under Development—would suffice simply because they are small enough to be able to make more drastic, swift changes without it causing as much disruption like it would within a larger organization.

At SNA, we have developed our own assessment to help our clients assess their Agility maturity based upon the following criteria, or attributes:

- Vision

- Maturity

- Lean Governance

- Innovation

- Coherence

- Flexibility

- Cost

- Speed

- Quality

- Reusability

Coherence

The third factor I've seen is coherence—that is, bringing the whole organization together on the same line, same page, and same goal. Coherence gets lost easily in any organization of any size but especially the larger the enterprise because each team is pursuing its own mandate, its own goal, and trying to achieve Agility in their own way. This means that even if there is an equal desire across the enterprise to be Agile, they end up running in different directions, creating confusion.

So there must be coherence not only among the leadership or within specific teams, but *between* teams. This sense of coherence should link back directly into the clear strategic vision so that it can be a unifying source, allowing each team and individual to see their role within the "big picture" of the enterprise.

Beyond these three foundational factors, there are other environmental factors that need to be considered within the context of Agility, including the following:

- Having good leadership who can promote and champion Agility within the organization

- High-performance climate in which everyone is trying to excel within their specific area/role

- Commitment to Agility from the top level to the operational level

- Connection between various business units to increase collaboration

- Freedom of choice among teams to be able to select the solution they want as long as it is within the guidelines that have been established for the strategic vision

And last but not least, there must also be openness, the kind of culture in which everyone can speak out and express their views with candor in a way that encourages innovation.

An entire book could be written just about these factors and how enterprises can develop them, but what is most important for our discussion is understanding that they can work together to help an organization reach the prerequisite level of maturity before embarking on their Agile journey. But one must keep in mind that the Agile journey is one without an end—there is no finish line but, rather, an infinite marathon of sprints to continually be better than the day before.

Bottom-Line Agility

To bring this back into focus, we'll return once more to Southeast Regional Bank so we can have a practical view of how all of this comes together and how Agility in three phases helps enterprises be thorough in their EA process and add value to the bottom line.

STRATEGY/PLANNING

Starting at the high-level enterprise view, their goal over the next ten to thirty years was to become a one-stop shop for banking services. Now there were a variety of drivers behind this goal, including business and technology drivers. On the Segment Level, we divided these up into strategic initiatives, such as "We need a CRM. We need an MDM. We need digitization. We need finance reporting to be streamlined."

From those strategic initiatives, we established goals for each one that identify the necessary implementation initiatives, such as building a digital customer information management solution. Once we identified the implementation initiatives, it was time to get into the actual implementation process.

IMPLEMENTATION

Before implementation could occur, we first needed to identify the requirements and design the requirements. Once they were designed, we coded them—or, depending on the initiative, purchased a cost product or SAAS solution. After the solution was built (or purchased), then it had to be tested by going into configuration management, a repository indeed for storing the code.

From there, a package was built for the code, which also required testing to confirm that the original initiative requirements were being met. Any defects found had to be addressed or fixed in the source code again. Once everything was done, the package was deployed into operations, where it became a service offer.

OPERATIONS

Services that are developed are offered to someone to consume, whether they are internal (i.e., staff) or external (i.e., customers). Even when you are offering them to internal teams, it is typical nowadays to say that they are being charged for the service you're providing, known as an IT showback. This means that even though they are not actually being billed for the service, it allows you to assign a cost to the service for informational purposes.

From an operational view, it shows the enterprise how much of the IT resources are being consumed in financial terms. By comparing the showback cost to what the cost would have been to consume a third-party solution, the enterprise can gain a clearer sense of the ROI for the solution that was implemented.

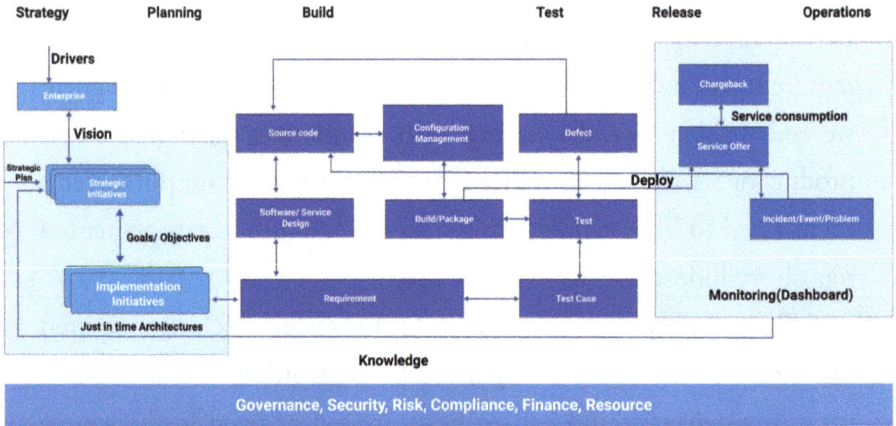

Until recently, IT resources have often gone unnoticed in the organization in terms of the cost benefit. Everyone looks at the cost of the service, whether they develop it themselves or they purchase it, but they have not looked at how all the departments are consuming those resources since there was no metric being used to help them assess the bottom-line value.

With Southeast Regional Bank, the EA process was not simply about streamlining and becoming Agile for the sake of being Agile but to guide them in how the Agile mindset could help them look at value, the return investment of the solutions being implemented to achieve their strategic vision.

As Enterprise Architects, we help measure these services and showback metrics during the Operations Phase to show where Agility is being achieved by the rearchitecting, or if there are any defects that need to be addressed that will improve both the organizational Agility and the bottom-line IT costs. Sometimes those issues will need to be addressed in the source code itself, or sometimes it may prompt a revisiting of the strategic initiatives. At other times they are defects that will get addressed in the next EA generation cycle, but the cost analysis and Enterprise Architect can help guide those decisions.

By having this understanding of how a business capability is planned, developed, and operated, we helped make the whole organization Agile. Therefore, this end-to-end model benefits the enterprise by providing them with a pattern to follow for future innovation, maintaining the Agile mindset as new solutions are implemented.

Constructing an Agile Culture

All this brings us back around to the role of the Enterprise Architect in guiding the organization through their new blueprint. Since the Enterprise Architect's end goal is to optimize the enterprise they are serving, this naturally includes building the capability for Agility.

This means establishing the right EA Team with the right roles and responsibilities that will encourage Agility, because while Agility is enabled through technology, it must be driven by management. To be driven effectively by management, there must be a level of buy-in in which the leadership understands the risks involved but is ready to face them. The Enterprise Architect plays a vital role in helping leadership assess those risks and gauge the maturity of the enterprise to face those risks.

> Since the Enterprise Architect's end goal is to optimize the enterprise they are serving, this naturally includes building the capability for Agility.

From a SAFe® perspective, this means leaders must drive the change from the front and build a corporate culture in which everyone is working to be Agile rather than blocking it from occurring. In a typical environment, enterprises use gated governance, in which each stage of development is guarded by quality gates and bureaucratic red tape. Some argue these governance quality gates are essential to ensure that the capabilities are aligned with the strategy, but too often this approach gets in the way of Agility occurring. While you absolutely need governance, the Enterprise Architect helps prevent the kind of slowdown in implementation that over-governance can cause.

Also, it's important to understand that while leadership involvement and buy-in are vital, that does not mean Agility is a top-down corporate approach in which actions are mandated to the working masses from the C-Suite. Rather, an Agile culture understands that because the frontline workers will be the end users most affected by the technology, there must be an inverted corporate pyramid in which the front line is at the top and the C-Suite is at the bottom, providing their full support. This can only be achieved when there is a culture in which feedback is valued from every member and in which there is psychological safety for workers to share their stories.

When that culture is present, there is less of a need for leadership to control people because the people feel personally invested in the outcomes, finding meaning in their work. That meaning must be centered in the customer and whether they are truly being served. Furthermore, when there is a higher level of communication and trust among people and teams, it frees the enterprise from a culture of slow, bureaucratic-style decision making and replaces it with decisions based in a clear vision of the goal and delegating responsibility.

The Innovation Framework

I would be remiss to close this chapter on Agility without discussing the concept of innovation as it relates to an enterprise adopting Agile principles. To properly discuss it, however, we need to be on the same page of what I mean by "innovation," as it is a word that is used in a lot of ways. In their book *The Game Changer*, authors A. G. Lafley and Ram Charan describe innovation in this way: "Innovation is the conversion of a new idea into revenues and profits."[7]

Likewise, management expert Peter Drucker once defined it as "the task of endowing human and material resources with new and greater wealth-producing capacity."[8]

In other words, innovation is not only about discovery of a new idea or method or even the technology itself but also being able to act upon it and take it to the market in a way that adds value to both the customer and enterprise.

With this in mind, innovation will look different in each enterprise and industry, and I believe the late Steve Jobs provided a valuable perspective when he said, "Innovation is saying no to 1,000 things." In other words, it's not innovative to try something new simply for the sake of trying. Rather, true innovation is composed of the changes you make that help the enterprise fulfill its mission and vision in whatever way will provide the highest value.

Therefore, a good idea is only one in which the organization can create business from it. From my perspective, this is the distinction between invention and innovation: *invention* is when you come up with something new, whether you take it to market or not. But *innovation* is when you take it to market and

> Innovation is not only about discovery of a new idea or method or even the technology itself but also being able to act upon it and take it to the market in a way that adds value to both the customer and enterprise.

---

7 A. G. Lafley and Ram Charan, *The Game Changer: How You Can Drive Revenue and Profit Growth with Innovation* (New York: Crown Business, 2008).

8 Peter F. Drucker, *Management: Tasks, Responsibilities, Practices* (New Delhi: Allied Publishers, 1974), 67.

can build business around that new idea. As I've tried to mention consistently throughout our discussion, the mission and vision of the enterprise must always come first in any decision or architectural transformation; therefore the same should be true for any innovations being considered.

Oftentimes, organizations pursue innovation by bringing together ideas from the employees on improvements they would like to make in a corporate-wide "brainstorming" initiative, shortlist a few of the ideas, and then select the best of the best to embark upon. They may even conduct market research or identify gaps within the industry to help them pinpoint which innovations to pursue. These approaches can be good, but unless the selected innovations are aligned to the mission and vision of the organization, they will ultimately prove unsuccessful.

Sometimes the organization may be embarking on a truly innovative idea but simply does not have the capacity to roll out those innovations in a proper manner. It then becomes something of a gamble as to whether the innovation will prove successful or not. To go back to the Jobs quote, then, innovation can be just as much about what you say "no" to as much as what you say "yes" to. Ultimately, it comes down to what is best aligned with the enterprise's goals and objectives.

TYPES OF INNOVATIONS

First, it's important to understand the types of innovations that an enterprise will encounter based on the overall long-term strategy. Regardless of their defined end goal, the enterprise must clarify its innovation strategy since this will dictate the architectural approach, whether Baseline First or Target First, as discussed in chapter 6. No matter whether it's a business or technology innovation, these approaches can be defined along a spectrum:

- Radical (Target First): This is when the innovation signals a major shift or disruption in either the existing technology or business models.

- Semi-Radical: When the innovation being considered is near to the existing business model but new in terms of the technology, then it would be a "Semi-Radical" innovation. Likewise, if it is near to the existing technology but new in terms of the business model, it would also be considered "Semi-Radical."

- Incremental (Baseline First): When an innovation is near to the existing business model or the existing technology, then it is considered an "Incremental" innovation.

There are many types of business or technological innovations that an enterprise may encounter and can fit within the radical category. During my research, I found a great article called "15 Types of Innovation,"[9] which details the various kinds of radical innovations that might be considered, including the following:

1. Incremental Innovation

2. Process Innovation

3. Red Ocean Innovation (Known market spaces, existing industries)

4. Service Innovation

5. Business Model Innovation

6. Sustainable Innovation

7. Frugal Innovation

---

9   Marc Heleven, "15 Types of Innovation," The Gentle Art of Smart Stealing, accessed March 12, 2022, https://thegentleartofsmartstealing.wordpress.com/types-of-innovation/.

8. Blue Ocean Innovation (Unknown market spaces, untapped markets, etc.)

9. Radical Innovation

10. Open Source Innovation/Crowdsourcing

11. Experience Innovation

12. (Im)possible Innovation

13. Disruptive Innovation

14. User-Led Innovation

15. Supply Chain Innovation

So from this "innovation buffet," if you will, the decision must be made on what specific type of radical innovation is going to be made. Based on that, you then develop the Target Architecture that will achieve the radical innovation.

For example, when Amazon first began as an online bookstore, it was a radical innovation, because it was implementing both new technology (the internet) and a new business model by facilitating online book sales in contrast to the established brick-and-mortar bookstore business model.

A semi-radical example would be Uber. In terms of technology, Uber was not terribly innovative because they were implementing existing technology solutions—that is, mobile apps and GPS technology. But in terms of their business model, they were disrupting the existing business model by allowing customers to directly hail a ride, cutting out the middlemen of car rental agencies or cab dispatches. Artificial intelligence innovations and blockchain could also be considered semi-radical since they are technological innovations occurring in existing business models.

In contrast, if the change is incremental in nature, then you must first understand your baseline and then define some incremental improvements that need to be made to achieve the Target Architecture, whether in technology or business model. An example of incremental innovation would be when an enterprise makes adjustments to their business model or technology that help them reach a more optimal state, like many of the situations we've discussed with Southeast Regional Bank. This is the most common type of innovation made within the EA process, which is why the role of an Enterprise Architect is to help steer the organization to the right type of innovation that can best achieve the established business vision and mission.

INNOVATION LIFE CYCLE

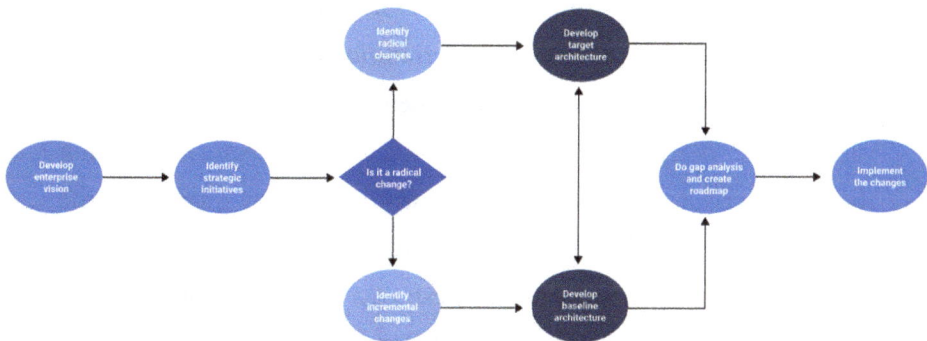

Beyond the types of innovations, an enterprise also needs to consider the life cycle they will go through in terms of innovations. As we saw in both the Scrum and XP processes discussed earlier, customer feedback should be instrumental in how an enterprise pursues innovation and is integrated into the life cycle of the innovation.

In working with enterprises in architecting their organizations in a way that creates an environment conducive to Agility and innovation, I've constructed an innovation framework (diagram above), which provides a clear avenue to help you narrow down the type of innovation your enterprise should pursue based on your specific situation and assess the best way forward.

As you can see, this framework begins with Vision to ensure that the business vision drives the decision-making process for innovation, because too often businesses allow an innovation to drive the vision. From that vision, you brainstorm your business drivers and your pain points, which will define some strategic, long-term initiatives.

From there, it works like a standard flow chart to guide leaders in recognizing whether the change needed is radical or incremental. If it is a radical change, then you must ask, "Are we approaching this from a business model perspective or from a technology perspective?"

While the diagram helps guide leaders, it's important to remember the role that the voice of the customer should play in the innovation life cycle as well. In the "old days" of the traditional innovation life cycle, organizations would only engage customers close to the end of the innovation cycle, delaying customer feedback until just before launching their new service or product. In other words, the only interaction the customer has with the innovation doesn't take place until it goes to market, when the enterprise wants to extract a profit from the customer.

Unfortunately, this customer engagement at the far end of the innovation cycle often means it's simply too late to implement any customer feedback. Or, if their feedback is implemented, then it could require a complete retooling of the new product or service in a way that ends up not being very cost effective for the business.

Instead, we encourage and utilize a customer-centric approach known as "Experience Innovation" or "Design Thinking," in which you are working to provide value to the customer and not only receive value from them in terms of revenue.

At its simplest, design thinking is a creative approach to solving problems and improving. It has becoming accepted standard practice over the past twenty years, and its effectiveness has shown it will continue to be so. What has made it so effective is that it is focused upon the human element of the problem, which makes it more customer-centric than other approaches that might focus only on process improvement or the technology itself.

Therefore, understanding the problem through design thinking requires an open dialogue with the customer to understand their perspective and experience. This can include "beta testing" a product or service with a selection of customers to identify areas of improvement for further innovation.

To gauge whether the changes are actually improvements, the enterprise assesses the answers to some key questions, such as the following:

- Is the solution being created actually desired by customers?

- Is it feasible to provide the solution to them?

- Is the solution viable in terms of providing them with more value than the cost to them?

- Is the solution sustainable over its expected product-market life cycle?

Furthermore, there are typically several standards to the development:

First, there is a Discovery Phase in which the enterprise is seeking to understand the problem and identify the consumer pain points from the human perspective, which can be done through market research and dialogue with consumers. Here, the enterprise is building empathy with the customer to truly understand their problem by asking questions about who they are and their specific needs.

In the second step, the enterprise takes all the information that was collected and generates some insights to define specific problems and observations. With that, the product team takes a third step to brainstorm and generate some solutions the customer could find desirable. There's lots of collaboration happening here to match ideas with the problems.

After this, the enterprise develops and designs possible solutions in a timely but cost-effective way. Which ideas from the previous step can realistically be developed? It doesn't have to be perfect at this point, but a prototype that can be tested.

And finally, these solutions are delivered and tested by customers in real time to generate their feedback in terms of the effectiveness. Based on that feedback, this cycle repeats back to the second step to define the customer response to the solution, and more brainstorming, prototyping, and testing is done until the best solution and product is designed.

With design thinking, the enterprise has an opportunity to learn directly from the customer, mitigate the risks that are assessed throughout the process, and then repeat the successes in future innovations through continuous conversation with the customer. Where the traditional life cycle looks at innovation as a one-way transactional relationship with the customer, design thinking looks at innovation as a two-way interaction, in which stronger relationships can be built with the customer—along with a stronger solution.

Typically, the mantra of innovation has been "Faster, better, cheaper"—that is, "How can we make our business/product/service faster, better, cheaper?" These are obvious driving factors for any enterprise wishing to remain competitive, but with an Agility mindset, a business has to cast a wider view that takes the customer experience into consideration.

Let's say an electronics company is designing a new mobile device; they must consider the right level of granularity for the customer experience. They cannot give over a microchip or circuit to the customer for their feedback—that would be *too* granular of an approach. Instead, they would need to hand over the entire device for accurate feedback on how the customer experiences the product. The level of granularity will differ from innovation to innovation, but providing the appropriate level will help yield both the greatest feedback and the greatest impact.

As an enterprise innovates in one area, they may be able to link those innovations to other areas of the business for further improvement. One example that comes to mind is how GE invented their first turbine in July 1949 as a gas turbine to generate electric power. But later on, they also incorporated the idea of the turbine into the washing machine in a "mix and match" approach to improve a completely different product. In this same spirit, an Agile organization looks for how they can "link" innovations across the enterprise to continuously improve products, services, or even processes. Making such connections, along with embracing new ideas and methods, helps the enterprise adapt and evolve over time. Meanwhile, businesses with an attitude of "We've always done things this one way" get left behind.

Beyond this, an enterprise must consider how extensively they are using new technologies and communication channels for both communicating with the customer and getting their feedback. For example, when the television show *The Office* was gaining in popularity early on in its run, NBC figured out that its greatest consumer base was among college-aged students. Therefore, knowing that their customers were online more than viewers of other popular shows at the time, they augmented the show's website, adding exclusive content, blogs, behind-the-scenes videos, and other content that would engage their target audience in new ways compared to other popular shows at the time.

Doing so even allowed them to get viewer feedback on plotlines and make adjustments to scripts they had not finished yet. This innovation proved successful, and other networks have since implemented similar strategies to engage with viewers. At its heart, extensibility boils down to what new experience you can bring to the customer.

Digitization

It's worth expanding a bit on this idea of digital transformation in both business and technology to look at how digitization is changing our world and creating innovations. In fact, I would argue that digitization is key to creating efficiencies, not only on the process side but also by bringing companies and customers closer together than ever before. One needs to look no further than the current state of the automotive industry to see the evidence of digitization, as vehicle components that were previously mechanical in nature have been replaced with computer-based components.

Returning to our previous example of Uber's business model, we see they used existing technology to "digitize" the taxi-hailing process directly from the customer's cell phone at any moment and from anywhere, without having to do any extensive planning ahead, make deposits, or perform other standard practices common to traditional taxis or car rentals. Through digitization, they've also allowed customers more control of the process by allowing them to request a specific size of vehicle, send a direct message to the driver to help make the pickup more efficient, and provide immediate customer feedback to the company on the quality of the ride in the form of a quick review.

To look at it another way, Uber used digitization as a means to eliminate the inefficiencies in the taxi-hailing and car-rental processes, thus innovating the customer experience. And by innovating the customer experience, they ended up innovating the industry itself.

Likewise, other companies can look at how technology can be utilized to transform the business-customer relationship and bring the two closer together, including recent changes in fintech. Banks have done this by allowing digital deposits from customer phones, eliminating the need for customers to wait in long lines at the bank drivethrough to deposit checks. Further efficiencies have been created by allowing customers to pay each other digitally through a mobile app.

Telecom is another industry that is being heavily digitized as analog methods become ancient history and the wireless war is waged. Many telecoms are even embracing a new framework that has emerged known as ODA (Open Digital Architecture). And even in food service, most restaurants nowadays have online menus set up so that customers can order directly through a mobile app for a pickup or delivery order, saving both the customer and business time from having to take the order over the phone.

By utilizing this innovation framework along with the principles of Agility, you can more accurately gauge not only whether your organization has an environment conducive for innovation but also whether you are considering all types of innovation. In today's market, the voice of the customer can serve not only as good PR for a company but also as a compass that lets the enterprise know whether they are headed in the best direction with innovations or whether they need to course-correct.

Conclusion

So how does an enterprise establish a level of governance that ensures the strategic vision is in place but without slowing down implementation? While tools and processes can certainly help an organization figure this out, this is a major contribution the Enterprise Architect can make. We keep an eye on how the implementation teams are doing, encouraging innovation in a controlled manner—what I like to refer to as "managed innovation." We want to encourage this managed innovation that follows a track on which it can be productive, rather than sporadic innovation that never takes root or leads to unintentional waste.

After all, innovation can't be expected to occur on its own, nor Agility to occur on its own. This is the hand-in-hand relationship that innovation and Agility have, in which Agility fosters innovation but in which innovation is managed in a way that encourages Agility. In that way, constructing an Agile culture is perhaps less of a science and more of an art.

Undergoing an EA process to optimize the business does not guarantee Agility, but approaching the process with an Agile mindset and Agile culture will serve to save time and resources on the road to Agility. Furthermore, the Enterprise Architect plays a role in bringing insight and balance to how the enterprise is achieving Agility and tracking innovation. At SNA Technologies, we are serious about helping enterprises pinpoint areas in their culture that need to be made more Agile for their EA process to be truly successful. After all, change cannot be made through tech innovations alone but must happen from the inside out.

In the end, Agility and Enterprise Architecture transformation become almost indistinguishable from one another when pursued correctly. The Agile enterprise is one that continuously seeks out the optimal way of accomplishing its vision, understanding that there is always a new horizon to reach for, implementing the solutions that will help them improve not only the enterprise itself, but its members, its customers, and, by extension, the world.

CHAPTER TAKEAWAYS

▶ Before an organization can become Agile, they must begin with a clear vision since Agile is the journey, not the end.

▶ Before an enterprise can become Agile, they must first raise their maturity level. Don't expect innovation to occur without first doing the prep work to become more mature.

▶ The Enterprise Architect plays a role in enterprise Agility through guiding managed innovation.

▶ The Enterprise Architect plays a role in establishing Lean governance through the LACE (Lean-Agile Center of Excellence) team.

▶ End-to-end Agility can be developed by utilizing the TopAgile Methodology, in which Agility occurs in three phases (Planning, Implementation, Operations) within all three architecture levels (Strategic, Segment, and Capability).

▶ The Enterprise Architect can help the enterprise assess ROI through IT showback metrics during the Operations Phase, providing further insight into the benefits of Agility.

▶ Agility alone does not guarantee innovation, but utilizing a framework for Agility can help an enterprise identify new innovations, especially through customer feedback and digitization.

▶ The innovation framework can be utilized to help an enterprise assess whether to pursue radical, semi-radical, or incremental innovations, along with design thinking and digitization to find areas of improvement and innovation.

CORE CONCEPTS TO MOVE FORWARD

When we began this discussion on Enterprise Architecture, I compared it with traditional architecture and presented it as a new blueprint for how enterprises can structure their vision and their work in an optimal way. But like all analogies, they eventually fall apart as you look deeper.

In traditional architecture, once the building is complete, that is it. There is little change to the physical structure taken after the ribbon-cutting ceremony. Perhaps modifications need to be made here and there over time—light bulbs changed, new coats of paint applied, leaky faucets repaired—but this is less about improving the structure and more about simply restoring it to its original condition.

Perhaps the architect is summoned by the business for a remodel job or constructing an annex. Even so, this is adding onto the original structure or making updates to it rather than reconstructing it.

So this is where Enterprise Architecture deviates the most from traditional architecture—it is not a one-time, finite activity but an Agile, ongoing process to continuously transform the business, making it the best it can be. While some EA projects will be more intensive and time-consuming in their scope than others, it is an ongoing evolution of improvement.

In that way, a better analogy for Enterprise Architecture is to view it not as a blueprint but more like a city plan, in which the city planner is looking at the city as a whole as well as its distinct units—business districts, downtown areas, residential areas, school zones, municipal properties—and continuously improving the city over time. After all, you can pick any major city, from New York to Tokyo, and it looks very different now than it did one hundred or two hundred years ago.

> While some EA projects will be more intensive and time-consuming in their scope than others, it is an ongoing evolution of improvement.

The city itself is the constant, even as it improves through new infrastructure, new housing developments, and new utility projects. While each of these capabilities will be accomplished by different workers and at different times, the city planner's job is to look at the entire scope of the city, putting the residents' needs first to make the city better with each passing day than it was the day before.

With this image in mind, the Enterprise Architect is like the city planner, looking at the enterprise as a whole, understanding its long-term goals, and aligning those goals with the best available solutions, whether those be IT solutions or otherwise. But the business mission must come first, supported by technology—not the other way around.

Certainly, this is a complex topic, and I would not be surprised if there are chapters and topics here that you need to revisit over time to better understand the concepts, whether you are a business leader or an aspiring Enterprise Architect. But we live in a world now where business and technology are inextricably linked to each other; therefore, understanding these concepts and putting them into practice under the guidance of an effective and certified Enterprise Architect can lead to improvement and innovation.

So with these last few pages, I want to remind you of some of the core concepts and key benefits of the EA process and of having an Enterprise Architect to guide you in that process. Every organization has an architecture, after all, whether they realize it or not. The question is whether that architecture is clearly designed, stable, and able to withstand change … or whether it is disorganized, weak, and susceptible to crumble in the face of change.

> The business mission must come first, supported by technology—not the other way around.

Enterprise Architecture Is a Holistic Approach

Enterprise Architecture should not be confused with general IT services, in which technology is the primary focus and driver. Rather, Enterprise Architecture looks at the entire enterprise, first from the business perspective, understanding the structure and needs of the business and its industry, and assessing what technology and tools will best support the business.

Enterprise Architecture Increases the Maturity of the Organization

Maturity has nothing to do with the age of your organization. You may be part of a one-hundred-year-old business, but if there is no singular vision, and there exist problems with communication, inefficient processes, and ineffective solutions, then it is an immature organization. Likewise, your enterprise may only be ten years old but have a very clear and stable Enterprise Architecture, making it a more mature organization. Maturity means being in optimal shape to do the work at hand, innovate, and meet challenges and changes in the marketplace.

Enterprise Architecture Increases the Organization's Agility

I will not say too much here about Agility since I devoted the last chapter to the topic, but it is important enough to mention again. Agile practices go hand in hand with an optimal Enterprise Architecture. Like a city plan, never ending in its scope, Agility is about ongoing action, not a final destination. Enterprise Architecture provides the framework, discipline, and practices that can help guide you into an Agile culture.

Enterprise Architecture Helps You Establish Strong Governance

As we've discussed multiple times throughout this book, the EA process helps establish principles and guides for building a structure of governance that creates consistency, checks and balances, and clear vision throughout the enterprise. Strong, Lean-based, Agile governance does not mean top-down mandates to the masses but continuous feedback among all levels of the organization to ensure that leadership provides the foundational support for the frontline workers. This approach has proven to help workers thrive in their respective roles and lead the organization to be better with each new project, initiative, and solution that is implemented.

Enterprise Architecture Helps You Define Innovation

Just because innovation is occurring within an organization does not mean that it is productive innovation or the right innovation that will drive the enterprise forward to fulfill its strategic vision. Utilizing an EA framework like TOGAF®—or others we've discussed—and having defined Architecture Principles help leadership know which innovations are the right ones to pursue. Just because a solution is the latest, shiniest new piece of tech on the market does not make it the best for your enterprise, so Enterprise Architecture helps you filter the solutions and innovations that will lead to true Agility.

> Just because innovation is occurring within an organization does not mean that it is productive innovation or the right innovation that will drive the enterprise forward to fulfill its strategic vision.

Enterprise Architecture Helps You Establish Strong Operations

A good Enterprise Architect encourages a system in which operations go beyond conducting the day-to-day work and become a part of the process of optimization. It encourages continuous feedback, in which stories from end users, whether they be staff or customers, are combined with analytical data to help dictate what further improvements can be made.

Obviously, the specific benefits of undergoing EA transformation will look different for each organization, depending on the scope of their work, their industry, and how mature the organization is at the beginning of the process. But the key benefits for any enterprise can be summarized as follows:

- Accelerates business transformation

- Drives strategic innovation

- Reengineers the corporation

- Manages complexity

- Manages change

- Manages Agility

- Reduces time to market

- Defines governance, risk, and compliance

- Optimizes the business processes

- Aligns IT to business

It is not an easy process, true, but few endeavors in the world that are meaningful and impactful could be described as "easy." EA transformation is for those organizations that want to move beyond the status quo and prepare themselves for long-term growth and Agility, no matter what changes occur—whether it is a transformation in the market, in technology, or when the next financial crisis comes along.

I founded SNA Technologies out of a desire to help make the process manageable and worthwhile. There are too many potential pitfalls, and there is too much risk, to go it alone. Instead, we hope to come alongside more enterprises, guide them in this process, and form long-lasting and mutually beneficial relationships that will not only improve the bottom line but also the lives of staff and their families and will meet the needs of customers around the globe. It is worth repeating our belief that if an enterprise improves, then by extension, the world improves too.

Like Enterprise Architecture, this discussion does not have to end here. Perhaps you still have questions about what this would look like for your enterprise. If so, I invite you to reach out to us on our website (snatechnologies.com) or email directly at info@snatechnologies.com so that we can have a specific discussion about whether your enterprise is ready for EA transformation. Perhaps you want to pursue a path to becoming an Enterprise Architect yourself. Likewise, I invite you to go through one of our courses, as we have a 99 percent success rate among our students pursuing TOGAF® certification.

When we each take ownership in our own part of improving the world through our work, then we can drive true innovation, no matter the nature of that work. What would a new blueprint or "city plan" accomplish for you and your team? What new levels of excellence could be achieved? I sincerely hope we can find the answers together.